CRAFTY CONCOCTIONS

101 Craft Supply Recipes
by Sue Hannah

 **Meadowbrook Press**
Distributed by Simon & Schuster
New York

Library of Congress Cataloging-in-Publication Data

Hannah, Sue.
  Crafty concoctions : 101 craft supply recipes / by Sue Hannah.
     p. cm.
  ISBN 0-88166-462-6 (Meadowbrook Press) ISBN 0-689-03018-5 (Simon & Schuster)
  1. Handicraft—Equipment and supplies—Juvenile literature. 2.
Artists' materials—Formulae—Juvenile literature. I. Title.
  TT153.7.H38 2003
  745.5—dc21
                          2003002514

Editorial Director: Christine Zuchora-Walske
Editor: Angela Wiechmann
Proofreader: Megan McGinnis
Production Manager: Paul Woods
Graphic Design Manager: Tamara Peterson
Art Director: Peggy Bates
Desktop Publishing: Danielle White
Cover Art and Illustrations: Blanche Sims

Published by Meadowbrook Press, 5451 Smetana Drive, Minnetonka, Minnesota 55343

www.meadowbrookpress.com

BOOK TRADE DISTRIBUTION by Simon and Schuster, a division of Simon and Schuster, Inc.,
1230 Avenue of the Americas, New York, New York 10020

08 07 06 05 04 03   10 9 8 7 6 5 4 3 2

Printed in the United States of America

Dedication

To my husband, Sean, for his love and support.

To my children, Kayla, Shane, and Katie:
You are my inspiration in everything that I do.
I love you all "to infinity and beyond!"

Acknowledgments

To all of the friends, family, and relatives who have contributed their wonderfully creative ideas to this book: You're the best!

To my mom, for introducing me to her own homemade crafty concoctions when I was a child and forever bringing out the creative side in me!

To Bruce Lansky: Thanks for giving me this wonderful opportunity!

To my editors, Christine Zuchora-Walske, Megan McGinnis, and Angela Wiechmann: Thanks for your excitement and encouragement throughout this entire project!

To the illustrator, Blanche Sims, for her wonderful creativity and talent.

We offer many more titles written to delight, inform, and entertain.
To order books with a credit card or browse our full selection of titles, visit our web site at:

www.meadowbrookpress.com

or call toll-free to place an order, request a free catalog, or ask a question: 1-800-338-2232
Meadowbrook Press • 5451 Smetana Drive • Minnetonka, MN • 55343

Contents

Introduction

You love using cool paints, clays, glues, and other supplies in your craft projects, right?

But what if I told you there's something just as fun as using cool craft supplies? What could it possibly be, you ask?

Making your own cool craft supplies, that's what!

Crafty Concoctions is jam-packed with 101 easy-to-read, step-by-step recipes to make all sorts of crafty concoctions—including crayons, paints, play doughs, clays, chalks, glues and pastes, inks and dyes, paper and paper concoctions, and more. You'll also find recipes for groovy body-art supplies and cosmetics, amazing special-effect concoctions for Halloween costumes, and delicious edible craft fixin's.

In addition, you'll find directions on how to use the concoctions in fun and creative ways. And as if that weren't enough, you'll also discover loads of tips, variations, and ideas for special craft projects you can make with your concoctions.

I know what you're thinking: *How can I possibly make craft supplies? It sounds way too hard!* It's quite easy, actually. All you need is a little creativity and some common ingredients found around your home or at your local craft supply store. You can make most of the concoctions for pennies, yet yours will be just as good as (if not better) than store-bought supplies.

Before you begin, please note there's one itty-bitty catch: It's fun to make these concoctions, but It's *educational* as well. (*Gasp!*) You'll learn skills such as pouring, mixing, measuring, cooking, baking, sculpting, molding, kneading, gluing, and grating. You'll also learn adding, subtracting, multiplying, dividing, problem solving, experimenting, and more. Don't worry, though. This type of learning will be a blast!

Enough said. The only way you'll know how fun and exciting these concoctions are is to try them yourself. Go to it! Just do it! Half of the fun (or maybe all the fun) is making them!

Safety First!

The activities in this book are designed to be kid-friendly and safe, but you still need to put safety first. Be sure to remember these guidelines:

- Whenever the directions say "Ask a grownup to help you..." do just that. Look for the special "Grownup Help" icon before you begin, then ask a parent, grandparent, neighbor, or any responsible adult if he or she could give you a helping hand. I'm sure any grownup would love to get in on the fun!

- Carefully read all the directions before you begin to make or use a concoction. Make sure you understand what needs to be done at each step. Always ask a grownup to help you with directions you don't understand. If you come across a material you don't recognize, take at look at the "What the Heck Is That?" section (see page x) or ask a grownup for help.

- Some craft supplies may look or smell good enough to eat, but remember that only the concoctions in the "Edible Concoctions" chapter (see pages 132–140) can be eaten. No matter how tempted you may be, don't eat or taste any concoctions other than those found in "Edible Concoctions" because they may make you sick.

- The best way to dispose of a concoction is to put it in a plastic bag and then toss the bag into the garbage. (But never throw any hot mixture into the garbage. Always let it cool first.) Also, many concoctions will clog drains, so never pour anything down the drain without asking for a grownup's permission first.

- Keep all concoctions out of the reach of pets and small children.

- Make this your motto: *It's better to be safe than sorry.* If you think a saucepan or bowl may be hot, use an oven mitt to grab hold of it—even if the directions don't specifically tell you to use one. If you think you need help with a particular step, find a grownup—even if the directions don't specifically call for adult supervision. Use common sense and be safe.

Expect a Mess!

You'll definitely want to expect a mess when making and using the crafty concoctions in this book. These pointers will help you keep the mess under control:

- The best place to work is on a kitchen table, kitchen floor, or patio table on a sunny day. Wherever you set up shop, cover the entire work area with newspapers, large garbage bags, an old shower curtain, or a plastic drop cloth. Remember that spills can splatter far, so the more area you cover, the better. Ask a grownup to help you with this step if necessary.

- Dress for a mess! Wear an art smock to protect your clothes, or if you don't have an art smock, make one. Use an old pillowcase (make sure you ask for a grownup's permission first) or a large garbage bag. Cut holes at the sides for your arms and a hole at the top for your head. To be extra safe, wear old clothes underneath the smock.

- Be sure to have plenty of old towels, rags, and paper towels on hand to wipe up spills, dribbles, and leaks.

- When you're done concocting for the day, clean up your work area thoroughly. Either throw away the item covering your work area, or wipe the covering clean, let it dry, and store it for later use. Wash the work area with soap and water to clean up any spills that the covering didn't catch. Carefully remove your smock and either throw it away or wipe it clean, let it dry, and store it for later use. Finally, wash your hands and any exposed skin that got messy.

What the Heck Is That?

As you glance through the recipes in this book, you'll probably come across a few items that make you think, "What the heck is that?" Here's a brief glossary of some of the less-common items you'll need to make your concoctions:

Alum: Alum is a spice used to keep pickles crisp. It can be purchased at a grocery store in the spice section.

Beeswax: Beeswax is mainly used to make candles, but it's also used in cosmetics, lotions, and balms. Beeswax comes in sheets or 1-pound blocks in a variety of colors and can be purchased at a craft supply store. One beeswax sheet, measuring 16⅝-by-8½ inches, equals about 6 tablespoons of melted beeswax. You can cut it into cubes with a butter knife. Never pour beeswax down the drain because it will clog it. Put the leftover beeswax in a plastic bag, then toss the bag into the garbage.

Borax: Borax is most often used to boost the cleaning power of laundry detergent. It's also used as a natural deodorizer, stain remover, and household cleaner. You can purchase borax at a grocery store in the laundry and cleaning supplies section. 20 Mule Team Borax is recommended.

Citric acid: Citric acid sounds a bit scary and maybe even dangerous, but it's not. It is perfectly safe to use. Some people use it to give lemonade that pucker-your-lips tart taste. It's also used in Kool-Aid and those sour candies kids love to eat. You can purchase citric acid at a drugstore and at many grocery stores.

Cream of tartar: Cream of tartar is used to produce a creamier texture in many sugary desserts. It's also used to stiffen beaten egg whites as well as to make baking powder. Cream of tartar can be purchased at a grocery store in the baking supplies section.

Epsom salts: Epsom salts are often added to a hot bath to help relax sore and tired muscles. They can be found at a grocery store or drugstore.

Flavor extracts: Flavor extracts add extra flavor to cakes, cookies, candies, and other desserts. Flavor extracts come in many flavors, including vanilla, orange, banana, almond, peppermint, and cherry, and they can be purchased at a grocery store in the baking supplies section.

Gelatin mix: Gelatin starts as a granulated mix, and it turns into a jellylike substance after you add water and let it set. You can find gelatin mix at a grocery store near Jell-O and pudding mixes.

Glycerin soap: Glycerin soap is used for making bars of soap. It comes in a solid form and is most commonly found in a 2-pound brick. It is soft and easy to cut using a butter knife. Glycerin soap can be purchased at a craft supply store.

Liquid glycerin: Glycerin is used in many consumer products, such as cosmetics and foods. It's often used to soften chapped lips and skin and is nontoxic. It comes as a clear liquid and can be purchased at a drugstore or at most grocery stores. Buy plain glycerin without added rose water.

Liquid starch: Liquid starch is a laundry product used to stiffen fabric. It can be purchased at a grocery store in the laundry and cleaning supplies section. You will need to ask for a grownup's help when using liquid starch.

Paraffin wax: Paraffin wax is mainly used to make candles. It can be purchased in blocks at a craft supply store. You can cut it into cubes with a butter knife. Never pour wax down the drain because it will clog it. Put the wax in a plastic bag and toss the bag into the garbage.

Petroleum jelly: Petroleum jelly is used for healing chapped lips and moisturizing dry skin. It can be purchased at a grocery store or drugstore. Vaseline Petroleum Jelly is recommended.

Plaster of Paris: Plaster of Paris is a powdered form of cement that hardens when mixed with water. It's often used to make molds, casts, and sculptures. It can be purchased at a hardware or craft supply store. Never pour plaster down the drain because it will clog it. Put the plaster in a plastic bag, then toss the bag into the garbage.

Tempera paint: Tempera paint comes in two forms: powdered or liquid. (You'll need one or the other to make some concoctions in this book.) It's a common paint that comes in an assortment of colors, and it's easy to use and clean up. Tempera paint can be purchased at a craft supply store as well as at many discount stores in the arts and crafts section.

Concoctions

Chunky Crayon

What do you do with those itty-bitty crayon pieces you find between your couch cushions and at the bottom of your crayon box? Recycle those broken pieces into a big chunky crayon!

Here's What You Need

8–10 brightly colored crayon pieces
¼ teaspoon vegetable oil
Nonstick muffin pan
Baking sheet
Oven mitt
Toothpick
Paper or other artwork
Crayon box

Here's How You Make It

1. Ask a grownup to help you preheat the oven to 275°F.

2. Remove the labels from the crayon pieces.

3. Pour the vegetable oil into a muffin pan cup.

4. Add enough crayon pieces to fill one-third of the muffin pan cup. If you add more crayon pieces, they won't melt evenly. If you use fewer crayon pieces, you'll get a thin crayon that will break when you use it.

5. Place the muffin pan on a baking sheet.

6. Ask a grownup to help you bake the crayon pieces in the oven for 4–6 minutes. Watch them closely because they melt quickly.

7. When the crayon pieces start to melt and blend, ask the grownup to help you use an oven mitt to remove the baking sheet from the oven.

8. Stir the crayon mixture gently using a toothpick.

9. Set the crayon mixture aside to cool.

10. When it's cool, pop the crayon out of the muffin pan.

Here's How You Use It

Use the crayon to color on paper or other artwork.

Here's How You Store It

Store the crayon for several months in a crayon box or wherever you keep your store-bought crayons.

Tip

It's easy to peel the labels from your crayons after you soak the crayons in a bowl of hot water for about 10 minutes.

Variations

- To make a solid-colored crayon, use similar-colored crayon pieces and stir well in step 8. To make a rainbow crayon, use different-colored crayon pieces and stir gently in step 8—don't overmix.

- Add ¼ teaspoon glitter during step 8 to make a sparkly crayon.

- To make an interesting crayon shape, use a heat-resistant metal mold instead of a muffin pan. Experiment with small animal-shaped molds. Use pink crayons in a pig-shaped mold or green crayons in a frog-shaped mold. Be creative!

Popsicle Crayon

If you've looked under the couch cushions but still can't find any crayons, why not make this cool crayon right at home? It even has a handle to make coloring easier.

Here's What You Need

Eight 1-by-1-inch cubes uncolored
  paraffin wax
Cheese grater
Tin can
Saucepan
Water
1½ tablespoons powdered tempera paint
2 Popsicle sticks
Oven mitt
Paper cup
Paper or other artwork
Crayon box

Here's How You Make It

1. Grate the paraffin wax using the smallest hole on your cheese grater until you have ½ cup of packed shavings.

2. Put the paraffin wax shavings in a tin can, then place the can in a saucepan filled with 1–2 inches of water.

3. Ask a grownup to help you place the saucepan on a stove burner and simmer the water on medium-low until the paraffin wax melts.

4. Stir the powdered tempera paint into the melted paraffin wax with a Popsicle stick.

5. Ask the grownup to help you simmer the mixture on low for about 5 minutes, stirring frequently.

6. Ask the grownup to help you use an oven mitt to remove the saucepan from the heat, then remove the can from the saucepan.

7. Ask the grownup to help you pour the mixture into a paper cup.

8. When the mixture begins to harden on top, stir it vigorously.

9. Wait 3–4 minutes, then place a clean Popsicle stick upright in the middle of the mixture. (If the Popsicle stick won't stay upright, wait about 1 minute and try again.)

10. Put the mixture in the fridge to harden for about 30 minutes.

11. Peel off the paper cup to reveal the chunky Popsicle crayon.

Here's How You Use It

Use the Popsicle stick as a handle for the crayon and color on paper or other artwork.

Here's How You Store It

Store the Popsicle crayon for several months in a crayon box or wherever you keep your store-bought crayons.

Fabric Crayon

Make an assortment of these funky fabric crayons, and color a permanent design on a T-shirt, place mat, or tablecloth.

Here's What You Need

6 similar-colored crayons
Tin can
Saucepan
Water
Oven mitt
Paper cup
1 tablespoon vegetable oil
Popsicle stick
Wax paper
White cotton fabric item (such as a T-shirt, place mat, or tablecloth)
Old dishtowel, iron, 1 cup white vinegar (optional)
Ziploc bag

Here's How You Make It

1. Remove the labels from the crayons.

2. Put the crayons in a tin can, then place the can in a saucepan filled with 1–2 inches of water.

3. Ask a grownup to help you place the saucepan on a stove burner and simmer the water on medium-low until the crayons melt.

Grownup Help

4. Ask the grownup to help you use an oven mitt to remove the saucepan from the heat, then remove the can from the saucepan.

5. Ask the grownup to help you pour the melted crayons into a paper cup.

6. Immediately mix the vegetable oil into the melted crayons with a Popsicle stick.

7. Stir the mixture every couple of minutes for 10–15 minutes until it's like putty.

8. Use the Popsicle stick to scoop the mixture out of the cup and onto a sheet of wax paper. Let it cool for 10 minutes.

9. Form the putty mixture into a log, then roll a new sheet of wax paper around it.

10. Let it harden in the fridge for about 1 hour.

Here's How You Use It

1. Use your fabric crayon to decorate a T-shirt, place mat, tablecloth, or any white cotton fabric. If you want to decorate a T-shirt, place a sheet of wax paper inside it to prevent the melted crayon from soaking through the cloth layers.

2. If you want to make your crayon design permanent, gently lay an old dishtowel over the design. (If you colored a T-shirt, leave the wax paper inside.) Ask a grownup to help you iron the design on the lowest setting for about 1 minute. To set the design, ask the grownup to help you run your item and a cup of white vinegar through a cold water cycle in the washing machine (don't add detergent or other clothes).

Here's How You Store It

Store the fabric crayon in a Ziploc bag in the fridge for several months.

Super-Slick Pastel Crayon

Use this pastel crayon to produce a rich, slick color in your artwork.

Here's What You Need

Four 1-by-1-inch cubes clear glycerin soap
Paper cup
Oven mitt
3 tablespoons powdered tempera paint
Popsicle stick
Paper or other artwork
Crayon box

Here's How You Make It

1. Ask a grownup to help you with this project. The melted soap can be *very hot.*

Grownup Help

2. Put the soap in a paper cup. Ask the grownup to help you microwave the soap on high for about 30 seconds. If the soap hasn't completely melted after 30 seconds, ask the grownup to help you continue heating it on high for 10 seconds at a time.

3. Ask the grownup to help you use an oven mitt to remove the mixture from the microwave. You should have about 4 tablespoons of melted soap.

4. Ask the grownup to help you use a Popsicle stick to stir in the powdered tempera paint.

5. Let the mixture cool for 1–2 minutes, then stir it again.

6. Place the mixture in the fridge to harden for about 1 hour.

7. Peel off the paper cup to reveal the pastel crayon inside.

Here's How You Use It

Use the pastel crayon to color on paper or other artwork.

Here's How You Store It

Store the crayon for several months in a crayon box or wherever you keep your store-bought crayons.

Sculpt 'n' Color Crayon

After molding this soft and squishy crayon into shape, you can use your finished creation to color your artwork.

Here's What You Need

Four 1-by-1-inch cubes beeswax
Cheese grater
Tin can
Saucepan
Water
Two 1-by-1-inch cubes uncolored
  paraffin wax
Popsicle stick
1½ tablespoons powdered tempera paint
Oven mitt
Paper cup
1 tablespoon baby oil
Paper or other artwork
Ziploc bag

Here's How You Make It

1. Grate the beeswax using the smallest hole on your cheese grater until you have ¼ cup of packed shavings.

2. Put the beeswax shavings in a tin can, then place the can in a saucepan filled with 1–2 inches of water.

3. Ask a grownup to help you place the saucepan on a stove burner and simmer the water on medium-low until the beeswax melts.

Grownup Help

4. Grate the paraffin wax using the smallest hole on your cheese grater until you have 2 tablespoons of packed shavings.

5. Ask the grownup to help you put the paraffin wax shavings in the can.

6. Use a Popsicle stick to stir the mixture until the paraffin wax completely melts.

7. Stir in the powdered tempera paint.

8. Ask the grownup to help you simmer the mixture on low heat for 2–3 minutes.

9. Ask the grownup to help you use an oven mitt to remove the saucepan from the heat, then remove the can from the saucepan.

10. Ask the grownup to help you pour the mixture into a paper cup.

11. Let the mixture cool slightly.

12. When the wax begins to harden on the top, mix in the baby oil and stir vigorously.

13. Let the mixture cool until it's no longer sticky.

Here's How You Use It

Mold the mixture into any shape you wish, then use the crayon to color on paper or other artwork.

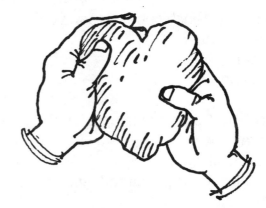

Here's How You Store It

Store the crayon in a Ziploc bag at room temperature for several months.

Soap Doodlers

For some good, clean fun, cook up this concoction, then doodle with your soapy crayons in the bathtub.

Here's What You Need

Two 3.1-ounce bars Ivory soap
Cheese grater
1 tablespoon vegetable oil
3 tablespoons water
Saucepan
Mixing spoon
2 teaspoons food coloring
Oven mitt
Plate or baking sheet
Wax paper
Soap and water
Airtight container

Here's How You Make It

1. Grate the bars of soap using the smallest hole on your cheese grater.

2. Place the soap shavings, vegetable oil, and water in the saucepan.

3. Ask a grownup to help you place the saucepan on a stove burner and heat the ingredients on medium-low. Stir the mixture constantly with the spoon until the soap melts and the mixture is doughy.

4. Mix in the food coloring.

5. Ask the grownup to help you use an oven mitt to remove the saucepan from the heat.

6. Spoon the soap out of the saucepan and onto a plate or baking sheet. Immediately soak the saucepan and spoon in hot water.

7. When the soap is cool enough to handle but still warm, knead it with your hands for about 1 minute.

8. Divide the soap into 4 sections. Or divide it into 2 sections for chunky crayons.

9. Using the palms of your hands, roll the soap into log shapes, then roll a piece of wax paper around each log.

10. Place the crayons on the plate or baking sheet and set them in the fridge to harden for about 1 hour.

Here's How You Use It

Color with the crayons on the bathtub walls. Be sure to clean your artwork off the bathtub walls with soap and water when you're done.

Variations

- Form the soap into balls instead of logs.

- Press the soap into individual sections of an ice cube tray or individual cups of a muffin pan to make chunky crayons.

Here's How You Store It

Store the crayons in an airtight container in the fridge for up to 1–2 weeks.

Basic Finger Paint

This simple concoction makes great finger paint, and because it contains soap, it washes up easily.

Here's What You Need

2 small mixing bowls
⅛ cup clear liquid dish soap
15–20 drops food coloring
Mixing spoon
2 tablespoons cornstarch
1 tablespoon cold water
Paper
Airtight container

Here's How You Make It

1. In one bowl, mix the dish soap and food coloring with the spoon.

2. In the other bowl, mix the cornstarch and cold water.

3. Add the second mixture to the first mixture and stir well.

Here's How You Use It

Using your fingers, paint the mixture on a sheet of paper.

Here's How You Store It

Store the finger paint in an airtight container at room temperature for up to 1–2 weeks. Stir the paint a few times before using it again.

Tip Small paper cups are great for holding finger paints. Place a different color of paint in each cup.

Washable Window Paint

On a bright sunny day, why not take the fun outdoors? Create a beautiful masterpiece for everyone to see on a window or a glass patio door.

Here's What You Need

⅛ cup clear liquid
    dish soap
3 tablespoons
    powdered
    tempera paint
2 tablespoons
    liquid starch
Small mixing bowl
Mixing spoon

Newspapers
Masking tape
Paintbrush
Washcloth and
    bucket of warm
    water or garden
    hose
Airtight container

Here's How You Make It

Ask a grownup to help you mix the dish soap, powdered tempera paint, and starch in the bowl with the spoon until the mixture resembles thick house paint.

Grownup Help

Here's How You Use It

1. Lay newspapers on the ground directly under your work area.

2. Use masking tape to frame the area of the window or patio door you want to paint.

3. Using a paintbrush, paint the mixture on the glass. You can even paint with your fingers, if you like.

4. When it's time to clean up, use a washcloth and a bucket of warm water to wash the paint off the window. Or ask a grownup to help you spray the paint off the window with a garden hose.

Here's How You Store It

Store the paint in an airtight container at room temperature for up to 1–2 weeks. Stir the paint a few times before using it again.

Scratch 'n' Sniff Paint

The best part about this paint is scratching it when it dries and sniffing the delicious scent.

Here's What You Need

Small mixing bowl
2 tablespoons Jell-O mix
1 teaspoon hot water
Mixing spoon
2–3 teaspoons liquid tempera paint
Paintbrush
Paper
Airtight container

Here's How You Make It

1. In the bowl, combine the Jell-O mix and the hot water with the spoon until the Jell-O mix dissolves.

2. Stir in the liquid tempera paint.

Here's How You Use It

1. Using a paintbrush, paint the mixture on a sheet of paper.

2. When your artwork is dry, scratch and sniff the paint.

Here's How You Store It

Store the paint in an airtight container at room temperature for up to 2–3 days. Stir the paint a few times before using it again.

Tips

◆ Choose a Jell-O flavor that complements the color of the paint you're mixing it with. For example, use grape Jell-O mix with purple paint or strawberry Jell-O mix with red paint.

◆ Although this paint may smell delicious, remember that you can't eat it.

Wonderful Watercolors

These watercolors are just as great as the expensive watercolor sets you find in craft stores. Do what the famous impressionist painters did: paint with your watercolors outside on a sunny day!

Here's What You Need

Small mixing bowl
1 tablespoon white vinegar
2 tablespoons baking soda
Mixing spoon
2 teaspoons cornstarch
1 teaspoon liquid glycerin
½ teaspoon food coloring
Egg carton
Paper cup
Water
Paintbrush
Paper

Here's How You Make It

1. In the bowl, mix the vinegar and baking soda with the spoon.

2. When the mixture stops foaming, stir in the cornstarch and glycerin.

3. Add the food coloring to make a dark, rich color. Mix well.

4. Pour the paint into a section of an egg carton.

5. To make a set of watercolors, repeat steps 1–4, using a different color of food coloring for each batch.

6. Let the paint harden overnight.

Here's How You Use It

1. Fill a paper cup with water, and dip your paintbrush into the water.

2. Dip the paintbrush into the watercolors, then paint on a sheet of paper.

Here's How You Store It

Store the watercolors in the egg carton at room temperature for several months.

Poster Paint

This rich paint is great for artwork projects that need thick coverage. You can use this paint for posters, signs, and other large projects.

Here's What You Need

2 tablespoons powdered tempera paint
1 teaspoon clear liquid dish soap
2 teaspoons liquid starch
Small mixing bowl
Mixing spoon
¼ teaspoon flour
Paintbrush
Heavy paper or cardboard
Airtight container

Here's How You Make It

1. Ask a grownup to help you mix the powdered tempera paint, dish soap, and starch in the bowl with the spoon.

2. Slowly stir in the flour. Mix well.

Here's How You Use It

Using a paintbrush, paint the mixture on heavy paper or cardboard.

Here's How You Store It

Store the paint in an airtight container at room temperature for up to 1 week. Stir the paint a few times before using it again.

Frosting Paint

You can apply this easy-to-make paint like frosting. It stays hard and puffy when dry. Just remember that you can't eat this paint—no matter how tasty it looks!

Here's What You Need

Small mixing bowl
½ cup cornstarch
1 tablespoon
  cold water
1 tablespoon
  cold milk
3 tablespoons clear
  liquid dish soap

5–10 drops
  food coloring
Ziploc bag
Safety scissors
Cardboard or
  heavy paper
Airtight container
  or Ziploc bag

Here's How You Make It

In the bowl, mix the cornstarch, cold water, cold milk, dish soap, and food coloring, kneading it with your hands until the mixture is thick and creamy. If the mixture is too thick, add 1 teaspoon of cold milk. If the mixture is too runny, add 1 teaspoon of cornstarch.

Here's How You Use It

1. Fill a Ziploc bag with the paint, then seal the bag. Cut a small hole in the corner of the bag. Squeeze the paint out of the bag to make designs on cardboard or heavy paper.

2. Set your artwork aside for 20–30 minutes to let the paint harden.

Here's How You Store It

Store the paint in an airtight container or Ziploc bag at room temperature for up to 1 week.

Crafty Idea

Make a pretend birthday cake out of a small cardboard box or plastic container. Decorate it with the frosting paint.

Shaving Cream Paint

Shaving cream makes a fun, foamy, and fluffy paint that leaves your hands feeling soft and smelling nice.

Here's What You Need

Small mixing bowl
1 cup shaving cream
1 teaspoon liquid bubble bath
Mixing spoon
2–3 teaspoons powdered tempera paint
Paintbrush
Wax paper

Here's How You Make It

1. In the bowl, mix the shaving cream and bubble bath with the spoon.

2. Stir in the powdered tempera paint.

Here's How You Use It

Use a paintbrush or your fingers to paint the mixture on a sheet of wax paper.

Here's How You Store It

This paint must be used up the same day you make it. It does not store well. Put any leftover paint in a plastic bag, then toss the bag into the garbage.

Marbled Paint

With this marbled paint, you can create attractive swirly designs to decorate your own gift tags, gift-wrap, or note paper.

Here's What You Need

2 cups liquid starch
Baking pan
1 tablespoon liquid tempera
   paint or acrylic paint
Popsicle stick
Paper
2 paper towels

Here's How You Make It

1. Ask a grownup to help you pour the starch into a baking pan.

Grownup Help

2. Slowly pour the liquid tempera paint or acrylic paint on top of the starch, but do not mix it in. The paint should float on the liquid. If the paint sinks to the bottom too quickly, mix 1 tablespoon of paint with 1–2 teaspoons of water and slowly pour the new paint mixture on top of the starch.

3. Use a Popsicle stick to swirl the paint gently, being careful not to overmix it.

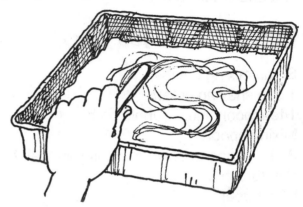

Here's How You Use It

1. Before the paint sinks, quickly place a sheet of paper on top of the mixture. Remove it after a couple of seconds, and the paint will have left a marbled design.

2. Lay the paper painted side up on a paper towel. Gently place a second paper towel on top of the design for a couple of seconds to remove excess paint.

3. Set the paper aside to dry.

Here's How You Store It

This paint must be used up immediately after you make it. It does not store well. Put any leftover paint in a plastic bag, then toss the bag into the garbage.

Crafty Idea

Make a gift tag by placing an index card on top of the paint mixture for a couple of seconds. Follow steps 2–3 in "Here's How You Use It" to dry the index card. When the paint has dried, fold the index card in half to make a gift tag.

Bubble-Print Paint

If you can blow bubbles, you'll have no problem making prints with this paint! You'll have fun making unique gift-wrap or decorative artwork.

Here's What You Need

Medium mixing bowl
1 cup water
½ cup clear liquid dish soap
¼ cup liquid tempera paint
2 tablespoons sugar
Mixing spoon
Shallow baking pan
Drinking straw
Paper
Bubble wand (optional)
Airtight container

Here's How You Make It

1. In the bowl, mix the water, dish soap, liquid tempera paint, and sugar with the spoon.

2. Pour the bubble mixture into a shallow baking pan.

Here's How You Use It

1. Place one end of a drinking straw into the paint mixture, then blow air through the straw to make bubbles. *Do not suck in the paint through the straw! The paint may make you sick.*

2. Gently place a sheet of paper on top of the bubbles for a couple of seconds. When you lift the paper, the bubbles will have left prints. Or dip a bubble wand into the paint and blow bubbles over the paper to create bubble prints.

Here's How You Store It

Store the paint in an airtight container at room temperature for up to 1 month. Stir the paint a few times before using it again.

shimmering crystal Paint

With this sparkling concoction, you can add a beautiful shimmering effect to your artwork.

Here's What You Need

1 tablespoon Epsom salts
1 tablespoon boiling water
Small mixing bowl
Mixing spoon
1–3 drops food coloring (optional)
Jumbo paintbrush
Paper

Here's How You Make It

1. Ask a grownup to help you mix the Epsom salts and the boiling water in the bowl with the spoon. If you want colored paint, stir in the food coloring.

2. Stir the mixture a few times until most of the salt dissolves.

Here's How You Use It

1. Using a jumbo paintbrush, paint the mixture on a sheet of paper.

2. Set the paper aside to dry. When the water evaporates from the salt mixture, shimmering crystals will appear.

Here's How You Store It

This paint must be used up immediately after you make it. It does not store well. Put any leftover paint in a plastic bag, then toss the bag into the garbage.

Crafty Ideas

● Brush the mixture onto holiday cards or pictures with snowy scenes to make them sparkle.

● Use black construction paper as a background for your artwork. When the salt mixture crystallizes, a night sky will appear, which would make a perfect setting for a spooky Halloween scene.

Shiny Paint

For a paint that looks wet and glossy even when dry, try this simple concoction. Your artwork will shine!

Here's What You Need

Small mixing bowl
1 tablespoon powdered tempera paint
2 teaspoons water
Mixing spoon
¼ cup corn syrup
Paintbrush
Heavy paper or a paper plate
Hard-boiled eggs (optional)
Airtight container

Here's How You Make It

1. In the bowl, mix the powdered tempera paint and the water with the spoon.

2. Mix in the corn syrup.

Here's How You Use It

Using a paintbrush, paint the mixture on heavy paper or a paper plate. You can

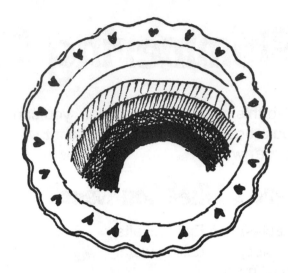

also use the paint to decorate hard-boiled eggs for Easter or other art projects.

Here's How You Store It

Store the paint in an airtight container in the fridge for up to 1–2 weeks. Stir the paint a few times before using it again. Also, make sure you store the decorated eggs in the fridge if you plan to eat them.

Variation

Stir ¼ teaspoon of glitter into the paint to make the paint sparkle as well as shine. Or sprinkle the glitter on top of the wet paint and let it dry.

Soapy Finger Paint Gel

This soapy, gel-like paint is perfect for finger painting. Make batches of finger paint in assorted colors, and have fun painting on paper or the bathtub walls.

Here's What You Need

¼ cup cornstarch
1½ tablespoons sugar
1 cup cold water
Medium saucepan
Mixing spoon
Oven mitt
1½ tablespoons clear liquid dish soap
15–20 drops food coloring
Plain paper or wax paper
Soap and water
Airtight container

Here's How You Make It

1. Combine the cornstarch, sugar, and cold water in a saucepan with the spoon.

2. Ask a grownup to help you place the saucepan on a stove burner and heat the mixture on low. Stir the mixture constantly until it becomes thick and gel-like.

Grownup Help

3. Ask the grownup to help you use an oven mitt to remove the saucepan from the heat.

4. Mix in the dish soap.

5. Stir in the food coloring.

6. Let the paint cool slightly.

Here's How You Use It

While the paint is a little warm, use your fingers to paint the mixture on plain paper, wax paper, or the bathtub walls. Be sure to clean your artwork off the bathtub walls with soap and water when you're done.

Here's How You Store It

Store the finger paint in an airtight container in the fridge for up to 4 days.

Crayon Melt Paint

This crafty concoction is like oil paint, and it leaves an interesting, rich finish on paper or even a T-shirt.

Here's What You Need

1 crayon
Tin can
Saucepan
Water
Oven mitt
1 tablespoon
   vegetable oil

Paper cup
Popsicle stick
Paintbrush or
   cotton swab
Paper

Here's How You Make It

1. Remove the label from the crayon.

2. Put the crayon in a tin can, then place the can in a saucepan filled with 1–2 inches of water.

3. Ask a grownup to help you place the saucepan on a stove burner and simmer the water on medium-low until the crayon melts.

Grownup Help

4. Ask the grownup to help you use an oven mitt to remove the saucepan from the heat, then remove the can from the saucepan.

5. Pour the vegetable oil into a paper cup.

6. Ask the grownup to help pour the melted crayon into the paper cup.

7. Use a Popsicle stick to stir the mixture vigorously until the ingredients are well blended.

8. Set the mixture aside to cool. Do not refrigerate it.

Here's How You Use It

Using a paintbrush, cotton swab, or your fingers, paint the mixture on paper.

Here's How You Store It

This paint must be used up immediately after you make it. It does not store well. Put any leftover paint in a plastic bag, then toss the bag into the garbage.

Paint a design on your favorite T-shirt:

1. Place a sheet of wax paper inside a white cotton T-shirt to prevent the paint from soaking through the cloth layers.

2. Use a paint-brush or cotton swab to paint a design on the T-shirt, then blot the excess paint with a paper towel.

3. To make your design permanent, leave the wax paper inside the T-shirt and gently lay an old dishtowel over the design. Ask a grownup to help you iron the design on a low setting for about 1 minute to melt the crayon into the fabric.

4. To set the design, ask the grownup to help you run your T-shirt and a cup of white vinegar through a cold water cycle in the washing machine (don't add detergent or other clothes).

The Greatest Dough on Earth

This classic play dough recipe has been in my family for many years. My kids like it much better than store-bought play dough because it's much softer and easier to work with.

Here's What You Need

Large saucepan
2 cups water
½ cup salt
½ teaspoon
  food coloring
Mixing spoon
Oven mitt

2 tablespoons
  vegetable oil
2 cups flour
2 tablespoons alum
Airtight container
  or Ziploc bag

Here's How You Make It

1. In the saucepan, mix the water, salt, and food coloring with the spoon.

2. Ask a grownup to help you place the saucepan on a stove burner and boil the mixture on high for about 1 minute. Stir the mixture until the salt dissolves.

Grownup Help

3. Ask the grownup to help you use an oven mitt to remove the saucepan from the stove.

4. While the mixture is still hot, stir in the vegetable oil, flour, and alum. Mix well.

5. When the dough is cool to the touch, knead it for about 5 minutes.

Here's How You Use It

Mold the play dough into any shape you wish.

Here's How You Store It

Store the dough in an airtight container or Ziploc bag in the fridge for several weeks.

Crafty Idea

To make a play dough porcupine, flatten the bottom of a big round lump of dough. Stick several 1-to-2-inch pieces of dry spaghetti into the lump of dough to make quills. Press on googly eyes to complete the porcupine.

Scented Play Dough

You'll love the smell of this deliciously scented play dough!

Here's What You Need

Large saucepan
1 cup flour
½ cup salt
1 tablespoon
  Kool-Aid mix
2 teaspoons
  cream of tartar
Mixing spoon
1 cup water

1 tablespoon
  vegetable oil
Oven mitt
Wax paper
Rolling pin and
  cookie cutter
  (optional)
Airtight container
  or Ziploc bag

Here's How You Make It

1. In the saucepan, mix the flour, salt, Kool-Aid mix, and cream of tartar with the spoon. Then stir in the water and vegetable oil.

2. Ask a grownup to help you place the saucepan on a stove burner and heat the mixture on medium, stirring constantly, until it's thick.

Grownup Help

3. Ask the grownup to help you use an oven mitt to remove the saucepan from the heat.

4. When the dough no longer feels sticky and is cool to the touch, place it on a sheet of wax paper.

5. Knead it with your hands for about 1 minute.

Here's How You Use It

Mold the dough into any shape you wish. Or if you want, roll the dough with a rolling pin and use a cookie cutter to cut shapes from it.

Here's How You Store It

Form the dough into balls and store them in an airtight container or Ziploc bag in the fridge for up to 1–2 weeks.

Apple-Cinnamon Dough

This fragrant dough is great for making crafts during the holidays or any time you want to enjoy a sweet apple-cinnamon scent.

Here's What You Need

Medium mixing bowl
½ cup applesauce
2 tablespoons white glue
  (such as Elmer's School Glue)
Mixing spoon
1 cup ground cinnamon
Rolling pin and cookie cutter (optional)
Drinking straw and string or ribbon
  (optional)

Here's How You Make It

1. In the bowl, mix the applesauce and glue with the spoon.

2. Mix in the cinnamon a little at a time.

3. Knead the dough with your hands until it's smooth. If the dough is too sticky, add more cinnamon. If the dough is too dry, add more applesauce.

Here's How You Use It

1. Mold the dough into any shape you wish. Or if you want, roll the dough with a rolling pin and use a cookie cutter to cut shapes from it.

2. If you want to hang your creation, use a drinking straw to poke a hole at the top of the creation before it hardens. Then loop a string or ribbon through the hole and tie the ends together.

3. To make your creation permanent, let it air-dry for 1–2 days, turning it occasionally.

Here's How You Store It

This dough must be used up the same day you make it. It does not store well. Put any leftover dough in a plastic bag, then toss the bag into the garbage.

Tip Though this dough may smell delicious, remember that you can't eat it.

Crafty Idea

Here's how to make an apple-cinnamon man ornament:

1. Roll the dough with a rolling pin and cut it with a gingerbread man cookie cutter.

2. Decorate the ornament by pressing raisins and candies into the dough. If you want to hang your creation, poke a hole at the top of the orna- ment with a toothpick or drinking straw before the ornament hardens.

3. Let the ornament air-dry for about 2 days, turning it occasionally. Loop raffia or ribbon through the hole and tie the ends together. Hang the ornament in a sunny window, on a Christmas tree, or in your parents' car as an air freshener.

No-Cook Play Dough

Here's a simple play dough that you don't have to cook—which means you can make it without a grownup's help.

Here's What You Need

Medium mixing bowl
1 cup flour
½ cup salt
4 tablespoons vegetable oil
Mixing spoon
⅓ cup water
15–20 drops food coloring (optional)
Rolling pin and cookie cutter (optional)
Airtight container or Ziploc bag

Here's How You Make It

1. In the bowl, mix the flour, salt, and vegetable oil with the spoon.

2. Add the water a little at a time until the mixture is doughy. If you want colored dough, add food coloring to the water before you mix the water with the dry ingredients.

3. Knead the dough with your hands until it's smooth. If the dough is too sticky, add more flour.

Here's How You Use It

Mold the dough into any shape you wish. Or roll the dough with a rolling pin and use a cookie cutter to cut shapes from it.

Here's How You Store It

Store the dough in an airtight container or Ziploc bag in the fridge for up to 2 weeks.

Salt Dough

Dish soap makes this dough soft, and salt allows your hardened sculpture to keep its shape for a long time.

Here's What You Need

Medium mixing bowl	4 cups flour
2 teaspoons liquid dish soap	Rolling pin and cookie cutter (optional)
1½ cup warm water	Drinking straw and string or ribbon (optional)
Mixing spoon	
½ teaspoon food coloring (optional)	Baking sheet
1 cup salt	Airtight container or Ziploc bag

Here's How You Make It

1. In the bowl, mix the dish soap and warm water with the spoon. If you want colored dough, add food coloring to the water before you mix the water with the dish soap.

2. Mix in the salt and stir until it dissolves.

3. Mix in the flour a little at a time.

4. Knead the dough with your hands until it's smooth.

Here's How You Use It

1. Mold the dough into any shape you wish. Or if you want, roll the dough with a rolling pin and use a cookie cutter to cut shapes from it.

2. If you want to hang your creation, use a drinking straw to poke a hole at the top of the creation before it hardens. Then loop a string or ribbon through the hole and tie the ends together.

3. To make your creation permanent, place it on a baking sheet. Ask a grownup to help you preheat the oven to 300°F, then bake your creation. Bake a thin cookie-cutter creation for about 10–20 minutes. A thicker creation might take up to 1 hour to harden. Check the creation frequently because it will burn if it's cooked too long.

Grownup Help

Here's How You Store It

Store the dough in an airtight container or a Ziploc bag in the fridge for up to 1 week.

Fizzy Fun Dough

For some fun, here's a terrific dough that will *fizzzz* in water!

Here's What You Need

Small mixing bowl
4 tablespoons citric acid
4 tablespoons cornstarch
½ cup baking soda
Mixing spoon
6 tablespoons baby oil
1 tablespoon liquid glycerin
8–10 drops food coloring (optional)
Cookie cutter or mold (optional)
Paper towel
Glass of water (optional)
Airtight container

Here's How You Make It

1. In the bowl, mix the citric acid, cornstarch, and baking soda with the spoon.

2. Mix in the baby oil 1 tablespoon at a time.

3. Stir in the glycerin. If you want colored dough, add food coloring to the glycerin before you mix the glycerin with the other ingredients.

4. Your mixture should look like cookie dough. If it's too wet, add more cornstarch. If it's too dry, add more baby oil.

Here's How You Use It

1. Form the dough into a ball or pack the dough firmly into a cookie cutter or mold.

2. Place the creation on a paper towel and let it air-dry for about 1 week.

3. When it's hardened, drop your creation into your bath water or a glass of water, and watch it fizz!

Here's How You Store It

Store the dough in an airtight container in the fridge for up to 1 week.

Confetti Dough

You'll love the bright rainbow sprinkles in this play dough. Squish it with your fingers, poke it, pound it, and use your imagination to make all sorts of brightly colored creations.

Here's What You Need

10 brightly colored crayons
Cheese grater
Medium mixing bowl
1 cup flour
⅛ cup salt
Mixing spoon
2 tablespoons
   vegetable oil
⅛ cup water
Rolling pin and cookie
   cutter (optional)
Airtight container or Ziploc bag

Here's How You Make It

1. Remove the labels from the crayons.

2. Grate the crayons using the smallest hole on your cheese grater until you have about ⅛ cup of shavings. Set them aside.

3. In the bowl, mix the flour and salt with the spoon. Stir in the vegetable oil, water, and crayon shavings.

4. Knead the dough with your hands until it's smooth.

Here's How You Use It

Mold the dough into any shape you wish. Or if you like, roll the dough with a rolling pin and use a cookie cutter to cut shapes from it.

Here's How You Store It

Store the dough in an airtight container or Ziploc bag in the fridge for up to 1–2 weeks.

Variation

Another way to grate the crayons is to break them into small pieces and roll them with a rolling pin until they are the size of finely chopped nuts.

Soft Soap Dough

You'll love cleaning up with this moldable, squishable soft soap dough.

Here's What You Need

3.1-ounce bar
  Ivory soap
Cheese grater
2 tablespoons
  vegetable oil
2 tablespoons
  water
Saucepan

5–10 drops food
  coloring (optional)
Mixing spoon
Oven mitt
Plate or baking sheet
Airtight container
  or Ziploc bag

Here's How You Make It

1. Grate the bar of soap using the smallest hole on your cheese grater.

2. Place the soap shavings, vegetable oil, and water in a saucepan. If you want colored soap, add food coloring to the water before you mix the water with the other ingredients.

3. Ask a grownup to help you place the saucepan on a stove burner and heat the mixture on medium-low. Stir the mixture constantly with the spoon until the soap melts and the mixture is doughy.

Grownup Help

4. Ask the grownup to help you use an oven mitt to remove the saucepan from the heat.

5. Spoon the soap dough out of the saucepan and onto a plate or baking sheet. Immediately soak the saucepan and spoon in hot water.

6. Let the soap dough cool for 10 minutes.

Here's How You Use It

1. Knead the soap dough with your hands, then mold it into any shape you wish.

2. If you want to make your creation permanent, place it on the plate or baking sheet and set it in the fridge for 30 minutes.

Here's How You Store It

Mold the dough into a ball and store it in an airtight container or Ziploc bag at room temperature for up to 1 week.

Shampoo Dough

Here's a fun, soapy dough that's great to play with—and it smells good, too. Three simple ingredients = tons of fun!

Here's What You Need

Medium mixing bowl
⅛ cup salt
1 cup flour
Mixing spoon
⅛ cup shampoo
Ziploc bag or airtight container

Here's How You Make It

1. In the bowl, mix the salt and flour with the spoon.

2. Add the shampoo and stir well.

3. Knead the dough with your hands until it's smooth. If the dough is too sticky, add more flour.

Here's How You Use It

Mold the dough into any shape you wish.

Here's How You Store It

Store the dough in a Ziploc bag or airtight container in the fridge for up to 1–2 weeks.

Dirt Dough

This dirty, messy concoction is perfect for making earthy-looking sculptures. Grab a shovel, head out to your garden, and dig up some fresh dirt—preferably without worms!

Here's What You Need

Large mixing bowl
1 cup fine, dry sandbox sand
   or beach sand
¼ cup salt
Mixing spoon
1 cup dirt
2 tablespoons white glue
   (such as Elmer's School Glue)
1–3 tablespoons water
Airtight container

Here's How You Make It

1. In the bowl, mix the sand and salt with the spoon.

2. Stir in the dirt and glue.

3. Add the water 1 tablespoon at a time and knead the dough with your hands until it sticks together. If the dough is too runny, add more dirt. If the dough is too hard, add more water.

4. Continue kneading the dough until it's smooth.

Here's How You Use It

1. Mold the dough into any shape you wish.

2. To make your creation permanent, let the dough air-dry outside or on a warm, sunny windowsill for 2–3 days.

Here's How You Store It

Store the dough in an airtight container at room temperature for up to 1 week.

Play Clay

This easy-to-make play clay hardens in a couple of days to a smooth, matte finish. It's perfect for making ornaments, necklace pendants, and other three-dimensional sculptures.

Here's What You Need

Large saucepan
2 cups baking soda
1 cup cornstarch
1½ cups water
Mixing spoon
½–1 teaspoon food coloring (optional)
Oven mitt
Wax paper
Rolling pin and cookie cutter (optional)
Baking sheet (optional)
Drinking straw and string or ribbon
   (optional)
Paintbrush and liquid tempera or acrylic
   paint (optional)
Airtight container or Ziploc bag

Here's How You Make It

1. In the saucepan, mix the baking soda, cornstarch, and water with the spoon. If you want colored clay, add food coloring to the water before you mix the water with the dry ingredients.

2. Ask a grownup to help you place the saucepan on a stove burner and heat the mixture on high, stirring it constantly. When the mixture starts to boil, reduce the heat to medium-low and continue stirring the mixture until it's like thick mashed potatoes and is difficult to stir.

Grownup Help

3. Ask the grownup to help you use an oven mitt to remove the saucepan from the heat. Stir the clay for 1 minute.

4. When the clay is cool enough to handle, scoop it out of the saucepan and set it on a sheet of wax paper. Immediately soak the saucepan and spoon in hot water.

5. Knead the clay with your hands until it's smooth. If the clay is too sticky, add more cornstarch.

Here's How You Use It

1. Mold the clay into any shape you wish. Or if you want, roll the clay with a rolling pin and use a cookie cutter to cut shapes from it.

2. If you want to hang your creation, use a drinking straw to poke a hole at the top of the creation before it hardens. Then loop a string or ribbon through the hole and tie the ends together.

3. If you want to make your creation permanent, air-dry it for 1–2 days, turning it occasionally. Or place the creation on a baking sheet and ask a grownup to help you preheat the oven to 300°F, then bake your creation. A thin cookie-cutter ornament might take only 15 minutes to bake, while a thicker project may take up to 1 hour to harden. Check the creation frequently because it will burn if it's cooked too long. You can paint your baked clay creation once it has cooled.

Here's How You Store It

Store the clay in an airtight container or Ziploc bag in the fridge for up to 2 weeks.

Perfect Plasticine

This concoction is similar to plasticine, an oil-based clay that doesn't dry out.

Here's What You Need

6 crayons
Cheese grater
Four 1-by-1-inch cubes beeswax
Tin can
Saucepan
Water
Popsicle stick
Oven mitt
1½ tablespoons petroleum jelly
Paper cup
Large Ziploc bag or airtight container

Here's How You Make It

1. Grate the beeswax using the smallest hole on your cheese grater until you have ¼ cup of packed shavings.

2. Put the beeswax shavings in a tin can, then place the can in a saucepan filled with 1–2 inches of water.

3. Ask a grownup to help you place the saucepan on a stove burner and simmer the water on medium-low until the beeswax melts.

Grownup Help

4. Remove the labels from the crayons. Ask the grownup to help you add the crayons to the melted beeswax.

5. Ask the grownup to help you stir the mixture occasionally with a Popsicle stick, until the crayons completely melt.

6. Ask the grownup to help you use an oven mitt to remove the saucepan from the heat, then remove the can from the saucepan.

7. Ask the grownup to help you immediately stir the petroleum jelly into the mixture.

8. Pour the mixture into a paper cup, then let the mixture harden in the fridge for 30 minutes.

9. Knead the plasticine with your hands until it's smooth.

Here's How You Use It

Mold the plasticine into any shape you wish and it will stay in that form.

Here's How You Store It

Store the plasticine in a large Ziploc bag or airtight container at room temperature for several months.

Quick Clay

Can't wait to see your finished art project? This modeling clay turns super hard super fast—in less than 15 minutes!

Here's What You Need

1 cup plaster of Paris
½ cup cold water
Large plastic margarine container
Popsicle stick
½ cup cornstarch
Plastic bag

Here's How You Make It

1. Ask a grownup to help you mix the plaster of Paris and cold water in a large margarine container, stirring the mixture with a Popsicle stick until it's creamy.

Grownup Help

2. Let the plaster of Paris set for 15 minutes.

3. Stir in the cornstarch.

4. Knead the clay with your hands until it's smooth.

Here's How You Use It

1. Mold the clay into any shape you wish.

2. If you want to make your creation permanent, let it air-dry for 10–15 minutes.

Here's How You Store It

This clay must be used up immediately after you make it. It does not store well. Put any leftover clay in a plastic bag, then toss the bag into the garbage.

Carving Clay

This carving clay stays soft for a long time, which makes it easy to carve. With a little practice, you can carve and create all sorts of things.

Here's What You Need

Safety scissors
Clean gallon-size cardboard milk carton
Petroleum jelly
2 cups plaster of Paris
1 cup cold water
Popsicle stick
½ cup white glue (such as Elmer's School Glue)
Several newspaper sheets
Potato peeler, plastic knife, or spoon
Airtight container

Here's How You Make It

1. Cut the milk carton in half horizontally. The bottom half of the milk carton will be the mold for your clay block.

2. Use your fingers to lightly coat the inside of the milk carton mold with petroleum jelly to prevent the clay from sticking.

3. Ask a grownup to help you mix the plaster of Paris and cold water in the milk carton mold, stirring the mixture with a Popsicle stick until it's creamy.

Grownup Help

4. Stir in the glue.

5. Let the clay harden for 1½–2 hours.

6. When the clay is hard, peel off the milk carton mold.

Here's How You Use It

1. Set your clay block on several sheets of newspaper. Carve your clay into any shape you wish, using a potato peeler, plastic knife, or spoon. Carve away from your face at all times.

2. If you want to make your creation permanent, let it air-dry overnight.

Here's How You Store It

Store the clay in an airtight container at room temperature for up to 1 week.

Bread Clay

Do you know you can make clay using a slice of bread? Check out this concoction to learn how to transform a simple slice of white bread into a piece of art.

Here's What You Need

Small mixing bowl
2 teaspoons white glue (such as Elmer's School Glue)
½ teaspoon liquid dish soap
Mixing spoon
White bread slice
Airtight container

Here's How You Make It

1. In the bowl, mix the glue and dish soap with the spoon. Stir the mixture well.

2. Remove the crust from the slice of bread.

3. Tear the bread into tiny pieces and add them to the mixture.

4. Knead the clay with your hands until it's doughy and no longer sticks to your fingers. If the clay is too sticky, add more bread pieces. If the clay is too dry, add more glue.

Here's How You Use It

1. Mold the clay into any shape you wish.

2. If you want to make your creation permanent, let it air-dry overnight.

Here's How You Store It

Store the clay in an airtight container in the fridge for up to 1 week.

Beadwork Clay

This clay is perfect for making beads for bracelets, necklaces, and other fabulous fashion accessories.

Here's What You Need

Medium saucepan
1 cup baking soda
½ cup cornstarch
Mixing spoon
¾ cup cold water
1 tablespoon vegetable oil
Oven mitt
Wax paper
Safety scissors
Drinking straws
Baking sheet (optional)
Small paintbrush
Liquid tempera or acrylic paint
String
Ziploc bag or airtight container

Here's How You Make It

1. In the saucepan, mix the baking soda and cornstarch with a mixing spoon.

2. Add the cold water and vegetable oil, stirring the mixture until it's smooth.

3. Ask a grownup to help you place the saucepan on a stove burner and heat the mixture on medium-low heat. Stir the mixture constantly until it's like thick mashed potatoes and is difficult to stir.

Grownup Help

4. Ask the grownup to help you use an oven mitt to remove the saucepan from the heat. Stir the clay for 1 minute.

5. Let the clay cool slightly, then spoon it out of the saucepan and onto a sheet of wax paper.

6. Immediately soak the saucepan and spoon in hot water.

7. When the clay is cool enough to handle, knead it with your hands until it's smooth. If the clay is too sticky, add more cornstarch.

Here's How You Use It

1. Roll small pieces of the clay into beads.

2. For each bead, cut a piece of a drinking straw a little longer than the bead. Insert a straw piece through the center of each bead to make a hole, and leave the straw piece inside. Trim the excess straw on either side of the bead.

3. Let the beads air-dry for 1–2 days. Or place them on a baking sheet and ask a grownup to help you preheat the oven to 300°F, then bake the beads for 15–20 minutes. If your beads are large, they may need to bake for a longer time. If they are small, they may not need to bake as long. Allow the beads to cool.

4. Use a small paintbrush to paint and decorate your beads with liquid tempera or acrylic paint.

5. Thread the beads onto string to make a bracelet or necklace.

Here's How You Store It

Store the clay in a Ziploc bag or airtight container in the fridge for up to 1–2 weeks.

Variation

For a glossy finish, cover your painted creation with a coat of clear nail polish.

Soap Carving Clay

Soap carving is easy and a lot of fun. With a little practice, you can create all sorts of interesting soap sculptures.

Here's What You Need

Two 3.1-ounce bars Ivory soap
Cheese grater
8 crayons
Tin can
2 saucepans
Water
Oven mitt
Mixing spoon
¼ cup warm water
Plate or wax paper
Plastic knife, potato peeler, spoon, or
  other carving tools
Airtight container

Here's How You Make It

1. Grate the bars of soap using the smallest hole on your cheese grater. Set the soap shavings aside.

2. Remove the labels from the crayons.

3. Put the crayons in a tin can, then place the can in one saucepan filled with 1–2 inches of water.

4. Ask a grownup to help you place the saucepan on a stove burner and simmer the water on medium-low until the crayons melt.

5. Ask the grownup to help you use an oven mitt to remove the saucepan from the heat, then remove the can from the saucepan.

6. Place the soap shavings and warm water in the second saucepan.

7. Ask the grownup to help you place the second saucepan on a stove burner and heat the mixture on medium-low. Use the spoon to stir the mixture until the soap melts and the mixture is doughy.

8. Ask the grownup to help you pour the melted crayons into the soap mixture. Stir the mixture well.

9. Ask the grownup to help you use an oven mitt to remove the second saucepan from the heat.

10. Spoon the soap mixture out of the saucepan and onto a plate or sheet of wax paper.

11. Immediately soak the saucepan and mixing spoon in hot water.

12. When the soap mixture is cool to the touch, knead it well with your hands and form it into a ball.

13. Place it in the fridge to harden for 1 hour.

Here's How You Use It

Carve the soap clay with a plastic knife, potato peeler, spoon, or other carving tools. Be sure to carve away from your face at all times.

Here's How You Store It

Mold the clay into a ball and store it in an airtight container in the fridge for up to 1 week.

Sand Sculpting Clay

This sandy clay can be molded and dried to make a permanent, stonelike creation.

Here's What You Need

Old saucepan or pot
2 cups fine, dry sandbox sand
    or beach sand
1 cup cornstarch
Mixing spoon
1½ cups hot water
Oven mitt
Baking sheet lined with aluminum foil

Here's How You Make It

1. In an old saucepan or pot, mix the sand and cornstarch with the spoon. (Don't use a good saucepan or pot because the sand will scratch it.)

2. Add the hot water and stir.

3. Ask a grownup to help you place the saucepan on a stove burner. Heat the mixture on medium, stirring it constantly, until it's like thick mashed potatoes and is difficult to stir.

Grownup Help

4. Ask the grownup to help you use an oven mitt to remove the saucepan from the heat.

5. Let the clay sit until it's cool enough to handle. Then place it on a baking sheet lined with aluminum foil.

6. Immediately soak the saucepan and spoon in hot water.

Here's How You Use It

1. Mold the clay into any shape you wish.

2. If you want to make your creation permanent, let it dry in a warm place or on a sunny windowsill. A large creation may take several days to dry completely.

Here's How You Store It

This clay must be used up immediately after you make it. It does not store well. Put any leftover clay in a plastic bag, then toss the bag into the garbage.

Here's how to make a sandcastle with this clay:

1. Use your fingers to coat the inside of a sand pail or sand-castle mold with petroleum jelly.

2. Pour the sand sculpting clay into the pail or mold, and let the mixture harden for ½–1 hour.

3. Place the mold upside down on a paper plate and let the sandcastle fall onto the plate.

4. Use a plastic knife to chisel windows, doors, or other features. Add shells, stones, flags, and so on to decorate the sandcastle.

5. Let your sandcastle harden for 2–3 days.

Snow Clay

With this concoction, you won't have to wait until winter to build a snowman—you can whip up some "snow" in your own kitchen at any time! When you're finished, your hands will be clean and your creation will never melt.

Here's What You Need

2 cups powdered laundry detergent
    (such as Ivory Snow)
⅓ cup hot water
Electric mixer
5–7 drops food coloring (optional)
Baking sheet, hard cardboard,
    or aluminum foil
Airtight container

Here's How You Make It

1. Ask a grownup to help you mix the detergent and hot water with an electric mixer.

2. Beat the mixture on high until it's thick and pasty. If it's too thin, add more detergent. If it's too thick, add more water.

3. Add food coloring if you want colored snow.

Here's How You Use It

1. Place the snow clay on a baking sheet, a piece of hard cardboard, or a piece of aluminum foil. Mold it into any shape you wish.

2. If you want to make your creation permanent, let it air-dry overnight.

Here's How You Store It

Store the clay in an airtight container at room temperature for up to 1 week.

● Mix a large batch of the snow clay to make a snow-covered mountain. Mold the clay into shape and sprinkle silver glitter on the top of the mountain so it will sparkle and shine.

● To make a snowman, make three balls with the snow clay. Use toothpicks or drinking straw pieces to hold the balls together as you stack them. Decorate the snowman with buttons and raisins.

Sidewalk Chalk

Turn your sidewalk into a canvas, and use these jumbo, chunky pieces of chalk to play hopscotch and tick-tack-toe and to draw pictures and roads.

Here's What You Need

2 toilet paper tubes
Masking tape, duct tape, or aluminum foil
Wax paper
¾ cup warm water
1½ cups plaster of Paris
3 tablespoons powdered tempera paint
Plastic margarine container
Popsicle stick
Paper
Ziploc bag

Here's How You Make It

1. Seal one end of each toilet paper tube with masking tape, duct tape, or aluminum foil.

2. To keep the plaster from sticking to the toilet paper tubes, line the inside of each tube with a piece of wax paper.

3. Ask a grownup to help you use a Popsicle stick to mix the warm water, plaster of Paris, and powdered tempera paint in a plastic margarine container. Stir the mixture until it's thick and creamy.

Grownup Help

4. Pour the mixture evenly into each of the toilet paper tubes. Let the plaster set for about 2 hours.

5. When the plaster is set, peel the toilet paper tubes to reveal the chalk sticks.

Chalks

Here's How You Use It

Use your chalk to draw or write on paper, a patio floor, or a sidewalk.

Here's How You Store It

Store the chalk for several months in a Ziploc bag or wherever you keep your store-bought chalk.

Variation

Besides using toilet paper tubes as molds, use candle molds, different-shaped containers, or muffin pans. To prevent sticking, use your fingers to lightly coat the inside of a mold with petroleum jelly before pouring in the plaster.

Crafty Idea

Here's how to make chalk shaped like an Easter egg or dinosaur egg:

1. Place the spout of a funnel in the opening of a large balloon. (Do not blow up the balloon.)

2. Making sure the funnel spout stays in the balloon, hold the funnel so the spout and balloon hang down. Spoon or pour the plaster into the funnel. Remove the funnel and tie the balloon directly above the plaster.

3. Set the balloon in a bowl of cold water to keep the egg from flattening on one side. Let the plaster harden in the balloon for about 2 hours.

4. Cut the balloon to reveal your egg. Immediately discard the popped balloon pieces into the garbage. If you like, use sandpaper or an emery board to sand the egg where the balloon was tied so it's nice and round.

5. Use your egg to write on the sidewalk.

Chalks

Easy Sidewalk Chalk

Here's a simple way to make chalk for some real sidewalk fun!

Here's What You Need

Medium mixing bowl
5–10 drops food coloring
2½ tablespoons warm water
Mixing spoon
1 cup powdered laundry detergent
Wax paper
Plastic wrap

Here's How You Make It

1. In the bowl, mix the food coloring and warm water with the spoon.

2. Add the powdered laundry detergent and stir the mixture well.

3. Form the mixture into a log and roll a piece of wax paper around it.

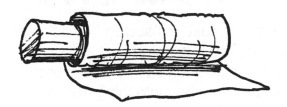

4. Place the chalk in the freezer to harden for about 1 hour.

Here's How You Use It

Use your chalk stick to draw or write on a patio floor or a sidewalk.

Here's How You Store It

Wrap the chalk in plastic wrap and store it in the freezer for up to 2 weeks.

Variation

Firmly pack the mixture into the sections of an ice cube tray. Place it in the freezer to harden for about 1 hour. When hard, pop the chalk out of the ice cube tray.

Squeeze 'n' Paint Chalk

You can make terrific 3-D artwork on a patio floor or a sidewalk with this squeezable chalk. Just squeeze 'n' paint!

Here's What You Need

Two jumbo chalk sticks
2 small mixing bowls
Warm water
Fork
½ teaspoon liquid dish soap

1 teaspoon flour
Plastic squeeze bottle or Ziploc bag and safety scissors
Heavy construction paper (optional)
Airtight container

Here's How You Make It

1. Soak the chalk sticks in one bowl of warm water for about 10 minutes.

2. Remove the wet chalk from the water, and place it in the other bowl. Use a fork to mash the chalk into a paste and break up all the lumps. You should make about 4 tablespoons of chalk paste.

3. Mix in the liquid dish soap and flour. Stir the mixture well. If it's too runny, add more flour. If it's too dry, add more dish soap.

4. Pour the chalk mixture into a plastic squeeze bottle. Or pour it into a Ziploc bag that has the tip of a bottom corner cut off, then seal the bag.

Here's How You Use It

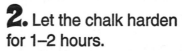

1. Squeeze and paint with the chalk mixture on a patio floor or a sidewalk. Or if you want, use it to draw designs on a sheet of heavy construction paper.

2. Let the chalk harden for 1–2 hours.

Here's How You Store It

This chalk must be used up immediately after you make it. It does not store well. Put any leftover chalk in a plastic bag, then throw the bag into the garbage.

Bright Stick

Here's a simple way to get a bright neon color from an ordinary stick of chalk.

Here's What You Need

Small mixing bowl
1 cup water
½ cup sugar
Mixing spoon
Colored chalk stick
Black construction paper or
  blackboard (optional)
Ziploc bag

Here's How You Make It

1. In the bowl, mix the water and sugar with the spoon.

2. Soak a colored chalk stick in the sugar water for 10–15 minutes.

Here's How You Use It

While the chalk is still damp, use it to draw on a patio floor or a sidewalk. Or if you want, use it to draw on black construction paper or a blackboard.

Here's How You Store It

Store the chalk for several months in a Ziploc bag or wherever you keep your store-bought chalk. To reuse this chalk after it has dried out, first soak it in water for 10–15 minutes.

Rainbow Chalk

With this variation of Sidewalk Chalk (see pages 53–54), you can decorate your sidewalk with a rainbow of color.

Here's What You Need

2 toilet paper tubes
Masking tape, duct tape, or aluminum foil
Wax paper
¾ cup warm water
1½ cups plaster of Paris
Popsicle stick
Plastic margarine container
4 paper cups
4 tablespoons powdered tempera paint in
   4 different colors (1 tablespoon per color)
Paper
Ziploc bag

Here's How You Make It

1. Seal one end of each toilet paper tube with masking tape, duct tape, or aluminum foil.

2. To keep the plaster from sticking to the toilet paper tubes, line the inside of each tube with a piece of wax paper.

3. Ask a grownup to help you use a Popsicle stick to mix the warm water and plaster of Paris in a margarine container. Stir the mixture until it's thick and creamy.

Grownup Help

4. Divide the plaster mixture evenly into 4 paper cups.

5. Mix 1 tablespoon of powdered tempera paint into each paper cup so you have 4 different colors of plaster.

6. Divide the plaster in the first cup evenly between the 2 toilet paper tubes. Let the plaster set for about 10 minutes.

7. Divide the plaster in the second cup evenly between the 2 toilet paper tubes. Let the plaster set for 2–3 minutes.

8. Divide the plaster in the third cup evenly between the 2 toilet paper tubes, then let the plaster set for 2–3 minutes.

9. Divide the plaster in the fourth cup evenly between the 2 toilet paper tubes, then let the plaster set for about 2 hours.

10. When the plaster is set, peel the toilet paper tubes to reveal the rainbow chalk sticks.

Here's How You Use It

Use your chalk to draw or write on paper, a patio floor, or a sidewalk.

Here's How You Store It

Store the chalk for several months in a Ziploc bag or wherever you keep your store-bought chalk.

Clay Chalk

Have fun molding this chalk into shape, and then use your hardened creation to create drawings and other inspired doodles on the sidewalk.

Here's What You Need

2 jumbo chalk sticks
2 small mixing bowls
Warm water
Fork
½ cup cornstarch
2 tablespoons liquid dish soap
Ziploc bag or airtight container

Here's How You Make It

1. Soak the chalk sticks in one bowl of warm water for about 10 minutes.

2. Remove the wet chalk from the water, and place it in the other bowl. Use a fork to mash the chalk into a paste and break up all the lumps. You should have about 4 tablespoons of chalk paste.

3. Add the cornstarch and dish soap.

4. Stir the mixture well and knead it with your hands until it's smooth. If the mixture is too dry, add more dish soap. If it's too sticky, soak and mash an additional half piece of jumbo chalk. Add the new chalk paste to the mixture and stir well.

Here's How You Use It

1. Mold the chalk into any shape you wish.

2. Let the chalk air-dry overnight.

3. Use your chalk to draw or write on a patio floor or a sidewalk.

Here's How You Store It

Store the chalk in a Ziploc bag or airtight container at room temperature for up to 1 week.

Window Chalk

Decorate your window with this thick, creamy chalk.

Here's What You Need

4 white chalk sticks
2 small mixing bowls
Warm water
Fork
5–10 drops food coloring or ½ tablespoon powdered tempera paint
1 teaspoon liquid dish soap
Paintbrush
Soap and water
Airtight container

Here's How You Make It

1. Soak the chalk sticks in one bowl of warm water for about 10 minutes.

2. Remove the wet chalk from the water, and place it in the other bowl. Use a fork to mash the chalk into a paste and break up all the lumps.

3. Add food coloring or powdered tempera paint to the chalk paste.

4. Mix in the dish soap to make the mixture thick and creamy.

5. Stir the mixture well.

Here's How You Use It

1. Use a paintbrush or your fingers to paint the mixture on a window.

2. When you're done, wash off the window chalk with soap and water.

Here's How You Store It

This chalk should be used up immediately after you make it. It does not store well. Put any leftover chalk in a plastic bag, then toss the bag into the garbage.

Homemade Glue

No more running to the craft supply store for glue. With this recipe handy, you'll never run out of glue again!

Here's What You Need

Small mixing bowl
½ cup cornstarch
¾ cup cold water
Mixing spoon
Saucepan
¾ cup warm water
2 tablespoons
　corn syrup

1 teaspoon white
　vinegar
Oven mitt
Popsicle stick
Artwork
Airtight container
　or Ziploc bag

Here's How You Make It

1. In the bowl, mix the cornstarch and the cold water with the spoon. Set the mixture aside.

2. In the saucepan, mix the warm water, corn syrup, and vinegar.

3. Ask a grownup help you place the saucepan on a stove burner and bring the water, corn syrup, and vinegar to a boil.

4. Ask a grownup to help you add the cornstarch and cold water to the mixture. Stir the mixture until it becomes thick and clear like petroleum jelly.

5. Ask the grownup to help you use an oven mitt to remove the saucepan from the heat.

6. Let the glue cool.

Here's How You Use It

Use a Popsicle stick to spread the mixture on the artwork you wish to glue.

Here's How You Store It

Store the glue in an airtight container or Ziploc bag at room temperature for up to 1 week.

Rainbow Glue

Cook up some colorful fun with this concoction. This gel-like glue creates a rainbow of colors.

Here's What You Need

Saucepan
½ cup cornstarch
2 cups cold water
2 tablespoons
    sugar
Mixing spoon
Oven mitt
3 small mixing
    bowls

5–10 drops red
    food coloring
5–10 drops blue
    food coloring
5–10 drops green
    food coloring
Large Ziploc bag
Popsicle stick

Here's How You Make It

1. In the saucepan, mix the cornstarch, cold water, and sugar with the spoon.

2. Ask a grownup to help you place the saucepan on a stove burner, then bring the mixture to a boil, stirring it constantly, until it becomes thick and clear like petroleum jelly.

Grownup
Help

3. Ask the grownup to help you use an oven mitt to remove the saucepan from the heat.

4. Set the mixture aside to cool for about 10 minutes.

5. Divide the mixture evenly into the three bowls.

6. Add red food coloring to the first bowl, blue food coloring to the second bowl, and green food coloring to the third bowl. Stir each well.

7. Spoon the colored glues out of the bowls and into a large Ziploc bag.

Here's How You Use It

Use a Popsicle stick or your fingers to spread the mixture on the artwork you wish to glue.

Here's How You Store It

Store the glue at room temperature for up to 1 week.

Peel 'n' stick Window Glue

With this glue, you can create some really cool designs to peel 'n' stick onto your window.

Here's What You Need

1 tablespoon unflavored gelatin mix
1½ tablespoons boiling water
Small mixing bowl
Fork
2 teaspoons liquid glycerin
1 teaspoon liquid tempera
   paint
Paintbrush
Plastic margarine container lid
   or plastic plate
Ziploc bag and safety scissors (optional)

Here's How You Make It

1. Ask a grownup to help you combine the gelatin mix with the boiling water in the bowl. Stir the mixture with a fork until the gelatin mix dissolves.

Grownup Help

2. Mix in the glycerin and liquid tempera paint.

3. Let the mixture set and cool for 1–3 minutes.

Here's How You Use It

1. Using a paintbrush, paint a thick design with the mixture on a margarine container lid or a plastic plate. Or if you want, pour the mixture into a Ziploc bag, cut off the tip from a bottom corner of the bag, seal the bag, and squeeze out a design onto the lid or plate. If the mixture gets too thick as you paint with it, simply stir in a small amount of hot water.

2. Let the design harden in the fridge for about 15 minutes.

3. Peel the design off the plastic lid or plate and stick it onto a window.

Here's How You Store It

This glue must be used up immediately after you make it. It does not store well. Put any leftover glue in a plastic bag, then toss the bag into the garbage.

Paper Paste

This sticky stuff is great for pasting paper crafts. Use it to paste pictures from magazines or newspapers into a collage.

Here's What You Need

Saucepan
1 cup water
1 tablespoon sugar
1 teaspoon white vinegar
½ cup cornstarch
Mixing spoon
Oven mitt
Popsicle stick
Artwork
Airtight container or Ziploc bag

Here's How You Make It

1. In the saucepan, mix the water, sugar, vinegar, and cornstarch with the spoon.

2. Ask a grownup to help you place the saucepan on a stove burner and heat the mixture on medium-low. Stir the mixture frequently until it becomes thick and creamy.

Grownup Help

3. Ask the grownup to help you use an oven mitt to remove the saucepan from the heat.

4. Let the paste cool.

Here's How You Use It

Use a Popsicle stick or your fingers to spread the mixture on the artwork you wish to paste.

Here's How You Store It

Store the paste in an airtight container or Ziploc bag at room temperature for up to 1 week.

stiff-a-Craft

This stiff concoction will harden fabric, bows, string, and yarn. Use it to make string sculptures and other stiffened creations.

Here's What You Need

Medium saucepan
2½ cups cold water
3 tablespoons sugar
½ cup cornstarch
Mixing spoon
Oven mitt
Cotton fabric item (such as string, yarn, a bow, or a piece of a bed sheet)
Wax paper
Balloon or mold (optional)
Plastic bag

Here's How You Make It

1. In the saucepan, mix the cold water, sugar, and cornstarch with the spoon.

2. Ask a grownup to help you place the saucepan on a stove burner and bring the solution to a boil, stirring frequently.

3. Reduce the setting to medium and heat the solution for 1 minute, stirring it constantly.

4. Ask the grownup to help you use an oven mitt to remove the saucepan from the heat.

5. Let the solution cool slightly.

Here's How You Use It

1. Select a fabric item you want to stiffen. The item should be 100 percent cotton or mostly cotton, such as string, yarn, a bow, or a piece of a bed sheet.

2. Completely soak the item in the mixture.

3. Remove as much excess mixture as you can by running your fingers along the item or by squeezing the item gently.

4. Set the item on a sheet of wax paper to air-dry overnight. Or if you want, drape or wrap the item over a balloon or other mold until it's dry and stiff.

Here's How You Store It

This mixture should be used up immediately after you make it. It does not store well. Put any leftover mixture in a plastic bag, then toss the bag into the garbage.

Variation

For extra sparkle, add 1–2 teaspoons of glitter to the glue mixture before soaking the item you want to stiffen.

Crafty Idea

Here's how to make a cool string sculpture:

1. Blow up a balloon and use your fingers to lightly coat it with petroleum jelly.

2. Pour the glue mixture into a shallow bowl.

3. Cut a long piece of thick cotton string or yarn and soak it in the glue mixture for a few seconds.

4. Remove the string from the mixture and remove the excess glue mixture by running your fingers along the string.

5. Wrap the string several times around the balloon in a random pattern.

6. Hang the balloon and let the string air-dry for 1–2 days.

7. When the string is completely dry, pop the balloon with a needle to reveal the unique sculpture. Immediately throw the popped balloon pieces into the garbage.

Colored Paste

With this colored paste you can make interesting designs and patterns on paper, gift-wrap, or note cards.

Here's What You Need

¼ cup wallpaper paste	Paper
Small mixing bowl	Newspaper
Popsicle stick	Jumbo paintbrush
1 tablespoon liquid tempera paint	Wide-tooth comb, brush, fork, stick, sponge, or rubber stamp
1–2 tablespoons sugar	Airtight container

Here's How You Make It

1. Ask a grownup to help you mix the wallpaper paste in the bowl according to the directions on the package.

2. Stir the paste with a Popsicle stick until it's smooth. Break up all lumps.

3. Mix in the liquid tempera paint.

4. Stir in the sugar and mix well.

Here's How You Use It

1. Set a sheet of paper on a sheet of newspaper, and use a jumbo paintbrush to cover the paper with a layer of the colored paste.

2. While the paste is still wet, use a wide-tooth comb, brush, fork, stick, or other object to scratch out a design in the paste. Or press an object, such as a sponge or rubber stamp, onto the wet paste to create a design. For some messy fun, try finger painting on the wet paste.

3. Let the decorated paste paper dry on the newspaper.

Here's How You Store It

Store the paste in an airtight container in the fridge for up to 2 weeks.

Funky Fabric Dye

Tie-dyeing was really popular in the sixties, and it's made a comeback today. With this fabric dye, you can create your own funky tie-dye tees!

Here's What You Need

2 tablespoons powdered clothes dye
1 cup hot water
1 tablespoon salt
Dishpan or bucket
Mixing spoon
Several large garbage bags
White 100-percent cotton T-shirt
Rubber bands
Rubber gloves
Baster (optional)
1 cup white vinegar
Plastic bag

Here's How You Make It

Ask a grownup to help you mix the dye, hot water, and salt in a dishpan or bucket, stirring the mixture with the spoon until the dye dissolves.

Grownup Help

Here's How You Use It

1. Lay several large garbage bags around your work area.

2. Wet the T-shirt with water so it's damp but not soaked. If the T-shirt is new, ask the grownup to help you wash it first and dry it until it's damp.

3. Crumple, twist, or fold the T-shirt however you like, and secure it with rubber bands in as many places as you like.

4. Put on a pair of rubber gloves and dip or soak the T-shirt in the dye mixture. Use a baster to drip the dye onto the shirt if you want more precise coloring.

5. Set the T-shirt on a large garbage bag.

6. Wait 1 hour, then remove the rubber bands from the T-shirt.

7. To set the dye, ask the grownup to help you run your T-shirt and a cup of white vinegar through a cold water cycle in the washing machine (don't add detergent or other clothes).

8. Hang the T-shirt to dry.

Here's How You Store It

This dye should be used up immediately after you make it. It does not store well. Put any leftover dye in a plastic bag, then toss the bag into the garbage.

Variation

Try tie-dyeing pillowcases, bed sheets, curtains, tablecloths, or fabric purses.

Fabric Ink

This waterproof fabric ink can be painted, stenciled, or stamped onto pillowcases or bed sheets. You can also use it to turn your favorite T-shirt into a piece of wearable art.

Here's What You Need

1 tablespoon powdered clothes dye
1 tablespoon hot water
Small mixing bowl or cup
Mixing spoon
1 tablespoon liquid glycerin
Fabric item (such as a T-shirt
   or pillowcase)
Wax paper
Paintbrush or rubber stamps
1 cup white vinegar
Glass jar with lid

Here's How You Make It

1. Ask a grownup to help you mix the dye and the hot water in a bowl or cup with a spoon until the dye dissolves.

2. Add the glycerin and stir well.

Here's How You Use It

1. Ask the grownup to help you wash and dry the fabric item you want to decorate.

2. If you're decorating a T-shirt or pillowcase, place a sheet of wax paper between the cloth layers so the ink won't soak through.

3. Using a paintbrush or rubber stamps, decorate the fabric with the ink.

4. Let the fabric dry for 1 hour.

5. To set the ink, ask the grownup to help you run your fabric item and 1 cup of

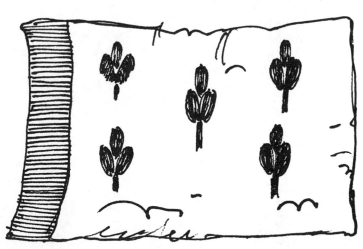

white vinegar through a cold water cycle in the washing machine (don't add detergent or other clothes).

Here's How You Store It

Store the ink in a glass jar at room temperature for several weeks. Stir the ink a few times before using it again.

Variation You can also use rubber stamps to decorate gift-wrap, note paper, or gift tags with the ink.

Eggshell Dye

Why spend money on expensive store-bought egg dye when you can make this simple dye for a fraction of the cost?

Here's What You Need

1 tablespoon
  white vinegar
1 cup boiling water
15–20 drops
  food coloring
Mixing spoon

Cup
Spoon or tongs
Hard-boiled eggs
Paper towels
Rolling pin
Glass jar with lid

Here's How You Make It

Ask a grownup to help you mix the vinegar, boiling water, and food coloring with the spoon in the cup.

Here's How You Use It

- To dye a hard-boiled egg, use the spoon or tongs to place the egg gently in the cup. Let it soak for 5–10 minutes. Remove the egg carefully, and set it on a paper towel to dry. Place the egg in the fridge if you wish to eat it later.

- To dye eggshells to use in mosaic projects, remove the shells from a hard-boiled egg, then rinse and clean them. Crush the eggshells with a rolling pin or break them into small pieces with your fingers. Soak the eggshells in the dye for 5–10 minutes, then place them on a paper towel to dry.

Here's How You Store It

Store the dye in a glass jar at room temperature for up to 1 week. Reheat the dye before using it again.

Variation

Put small stickers on the hard-boiled eggs or wrap several rubber bands around the eggs before they are dipped in the dye. When the eggs are completely dry, peel off the stickers or remove the rubber bands to reveal interesting decorations.

Stamp Pad Ink

This homemade stamp pad ink is easy to make, and you can even choose your own scented ink colors.

Here's What You Need

Small mixing bowl or cup
2 packages Kool-Aid mix
½ teaspoon hot water
2 tablespoons liquid glycerin
Mixing spoon
Stamp pad, paper plate,
   or Styrofoam meat tray
Rubber stamp
Paper item (such as note paper
   or gift-wrap)
Airtight stamp pad container
   or glass jar with lid

Here's How You Make It

In a bowl or cup, combine the Kool-Aid mix, hot water, and glycerin with the spoon. Mix until it's smooth.

Here's How You Use It

Pour the ink on a stamp pad, paper plate, or Styrofoam meat tray. Press a rubber stamp into the ink and then onto your paper.

Here's How You Store It

Store the ink in an airtight stamp pad container or glass jar at room temperature for several weeks.

Tip

To make a simple stamp pad for your ink, use a plastic margarine container or other plastic container with a lid. Cut a sponge or piece of foam rubber to fit in the bottom of the container. Moisten the sponge or foam rubber with a small amount of water and then pour your ink on it. Keep the container covered tightly when you're not using it.

Veggie Dye

Early pioneers extracted pigments from vegetables and other natural sources to create their own dyes. You can use these same veggie dyes to create a to-dye-for masterpiece.

Here's What You Need

½ cup red-onion skins, beets, carrots, or spinach
Saucepan
Water
Oven mitt
1 teaspoon white vinegar
Strainer
Glass jar with lid
Paintbrush
White paper
Plastic bag
Shallow dishpan (optional)
Paper towel

Here's How You Make It

1. Ask a grownup to help you chop one of the vegetables listed above into small pieces and place them in a saucepan. (Red-onion skins will make pink dye; beets will make dark pink dye; carrots will make orange dye; and spinach will make green dye.)

Grownup Help

2. Add enough water to the saucepan to cover the pieces.

3. Ask the grownup to help you place the saucepan on a stove burner, bring the water to a boil, then let it simmer over medium-low heat for 15–20 minutes or until the liquid is a dark, rich color.

4. Ask the grownup to help you use an oven mitt to remove the saucepan from the heat.

5. Add the vinegar to the colored liquid.

6. Allow the dye to cool, then pour it through a strainer and into a glass jar.

7. Put the leftover vegetable pulp in a plastic bag and toss the bag into the garbage.

Here's How You Use It

1. Paint with the dye on a sheet of white paper. Or if you want, color the paper by pouring the dye into a dishpan and dipping or soaking the paper in it.

2. Set your artwork on a paper towel to dry.

Here's How You Store It

Store the dye in the glass jar in the fridge for up to 1 week.

Crafty Idea

Soak dry pasta in the dye for 5–10 minutes. Set the colored pasta on paper towels to dry. Thread the colored pasta onto string or yarn to make pretty bracelets and necklaces, or glue the colored pasta onto paper to make a collage.

Flower Power Dye

Brightly colored flower petals produce beautiful, vibrant dyes. Use these natural dyes as watercolor paints.

Here's What You Need

½–1 cup brightly colored flower petals	Glass jar with lid
	Plastic bag
	Paintbrush
Saucepan	White paper
Water	Shallow dishpan (optional)
Oven mitt	
Strainer	Paper towel

Here's How You Make It

1. Ask a grownup to help you chop the flower petals into small pieces and place them in a saucepan.

Grownup Help

2. Add enough water to the saucepan to cover the petals.

3. Ask the grownup help you place the saucepan on a stove burner, bring the water to a boil, then let it simmer over medium-low heat for 15–20 minutes until the liquid is a dark, rich color.

4. Ask the grownup to help you use an oven mitt to remove the saucepan from the heat.

5. Allow the dye to cool, then pour it through a strainer and into a glass jar.

6. Put the leftover petal pulp in a plastic bag and toss the bag into the garbage.

Here's How You Use It

1. Paint with the dye on a sheet of white paper. Or if you want, color the paper by pouring the dye into a shallow dishpan and dipping or soaking the paper in it.

2. Set your artwork on a paper towel to dry.

Here's How You Store It

Store the dye in the glass jar in the fridge for up to 1 week.

Magical Color Dye

You can use this magical dye to color paper and then make the color change right before your eyes. Presto!

Here's What You Need

½ red cabbage
Large pot
Water
Mixing spoon
Oven mitt
Strainer
Shallow dishpan
Plastic bag
White paper

Paper towel
Cotton swabs
1 tablespoon white vinegar
2 small cups
1 teaspoon baking soda
½ teaspoon water
Glass jar with lid

Here's How You Make It

1. Ask a grownup to help you chop half of a red cabbage into small chunks and place them in a large pot.

2. Add enough water to the pot to cover the cabbage.

3. Ask the grownup to help you set the pot on a stove burner and bring the water to a boil. Stir the liquid constantly until the cabbage begins to lose its color.

4. Ask the grownup to help you use an oven mitt to remove the pot from the heat.

5. Allow the cabbage to soak in the water for about 15 minutes.

6. Use a strainer to strain the liquid into a shallow dishpan.

7. Put the leftover cabbage in a plastic bag and toss the bag into the garbage.

Here's How You Use It

1. Place a sheet of white paper into the dishpan, and let it soak in the dye for about 1 hour.

2. Remove the paper and set it on a paper towel to dry.

3. When the paper is dry, pour the vinegar into a cup. Dip a cotton swab in the vinegar and paint with it on the colored paper. Watch the color change magically right before your eyes!

4. Mix the baking soda and a ½ teaspoon of water in another cup. Use another cotton swab to paint the mixture on the colored paper, wait a couple of minutes, and watch the color change again!

Here's How You Store It

Store the dye in a glass jar in the fridge for up to 1 week.

Berry Good Ink

Berries are loaded with deep, rich colors, which is why they've been used for centuries to create ink. Use this "berry" good ink to create decorative artwork.

Here's What You Need

Strainer
Mixing bowl
½ cup ripe berries (such as raspberries, cranberries, blackberries, blueberries, or cherries)
Potato masher or fork
Plastic bag
1 teaspoon white vinegar
½ teaspoon salt
½ teaspoon water
Mixing spoon
Stamp pad and rubber stamp
Paper
Toothpick, cotton swab, or paintbrush and paper (optional)
Airtight stamp pad container or glass jar with lid

Here's How You Make It

1. Set a strainer on top of the bowl, and pour the berries into the strainer.

2. Use a potato masher or fork to mash the berries against the strainer until 2–3 tablespoons of berry juice drain into the bowl. You can also squeeze small handfuls of the berries with your hands to release the juice, if you wish.

3. Put the leftover pulp from the berries in a plastic bag and throw the bag into the garbage.

4. Add the vinegar, salt, and water to the berry juice. Stir the mixture.

Here's How You Use It

Pour the ink over a stamp pad. Press a stamp into the ink and then onto your paper. Or if you want, use a toothpick, cotton swab, or paintbrush to paint with the ink on paper.

Here's How You Store It

Store the ink in an airtight stamp pad container or glass jar at room temperature for several weeks.

Coffee Dye

This dye can be used to make ordinary white paper look really old. Use it to create an ancient treasure map leading to hidden booty.

Here's What You Need

1 cup strong black coffee (without cream or sugar)
Shallow dishpan
1 teaspoon white vinegar
¼ teaspoon salt
Mixing spoon
White paper
Clothespins and clothesline or newspaper
Airtight container

Here's How You Make It

1. Ask a grownup for a cup of strong black coffee (hot or cold). Pour it into the dishpan.

2. Add the vinegar and salt to the coffee and stir the mixture well with the spoon.

Here's How You Use It

1. Lay a sheet of white paper in the coffee mixture and let it soak for 20–30 minutes.

2. Hang the paper with clothespins on a clothesline or lay it on a sheet of newspaper to dry.

Here's How You Store It

Store the coffee dye in an airtight container at room temperature for up to 1 week.

Basic Paper

Using simple materials, you can make handmade sheets of paper right in your own home! Note: Be sure to learn how to make Basic Paper before you go on to other papermaking activities in this chapter.

Here's What You Need

8-by-10-inch wooden picture frame
Fine mesh or nylon netting
Thumbtacks or staple gun
Newspapers
Waste paper scraps (such as plain paper, paper napkins, paper towels, cereal boxes, junk mail, greeting cards, index cards, paper bags, tissue paper, toilet paper, facial tissues, and gift-wrap)
Large mixing bowl
2 cups warm water
Blender
Dishpan or baking pan (large enough to hold the picture frame)
Terry cloth towel
Damp sponge
Rags and sponges
Rolling pin
Airtight container

Here's How You Make It

1. First you must make a paper-making screen. Ask a grownup to help you with this step.

A. Remove the glass and backing from the picture frame.

B. Stretch a piece of fine mesh or nylon netting tightly over the frame, and ask the grownup to help you secure it to the frame with thumb-tacks or a staple gun.

2. Cover your work area with a few sheets of newspaper. Choose one or more of the listed waste paper scraps, and tear them into 1 cup of quarter-size pieces. (Be sure to remove any staples first.)

3. Place the paper pieces in the bowl and cover them with the warm water. Let them soak for about 1 hour.

4. Ask a grownup to help you place the paper pieces and the warm water in a blender. Fill the blender no more than two-thirds full. Also, make sure  there's about 2 parts water to 1 part paper, or you'll ruin the blender. With heavier paper scraps, such as construction paper or cardboard egg cartons, add an additional ½–1 cup of warm water.

5. Blend the paper pieces and warm water for about 2 minutes until the pulp is soupy and it has no chunks.

6. Fill the dishpan or baking pan half-full of water, and hold your papermaking screen on the surface of the water.

7. While still holding the screen, pour enough pulp on top of the screen to cover its entire surface.

8. Shake the screen gently from side to side to spread the pulp evenly over the screen.

9. Lift the screen from the water, and let it drain over the dishpan or baking pan for about 5 minutes.

10. Flip the screen over so the pulp falls onto a terry cloth towel. If the pulp doesn't fall off the screen, pat the back of the screen with a damp sponge.

11. Carefully fold the towel over and on top of the pulp.

12. Take the towel and pulp outdoors or have plenty of rags and sponges handy. Roll a rolling pin over the towel and pulp, pressing firmly to squeeze as much water as you can from the pulp.

13. Slowly unfold the towel. Let the towel and pulp dry in a warm place.

14. When the paper is dry, peel it off the towel.

15. You will have enough leftover pulp to make several sheets of paper. Repeat steps 6–14 for each sheet you wish to make.

Here's How You Use It

Use your homemade paper to make artwork and crafts, such as note cards, greeting cards, gift tags, bookmarks, thank-you notes, and more.

Here's How You Store It

Store the pulp in an airtight container in the fridge up to 4 days.

Tips

◆ The color and texture of your finished sheet of paper will depend on the type of paper scraps you use. This makes papermaking interesting because you never know what the final result will be!

◆ Don't use newspaper or any paper with a lot of black print as scrap material, or your paper will appear dirty and gray.

◆ Once you master the basic papermaking process, you can move on to the other paper concoctions.

Variations

● If you're making only one sheet of paper, you can let the pulp dry directly on the screen without flipping it onto a towel. Carefully peel your sheet of paper off the screen while the paper is slightly damp. Set it aside to dry completely.

● Use the top portion of a pair of nylon pantyhose in place of mesh or netting to make your papermaking screen. Stretch the pantyhose tightly over the picture frame. Cut off the legs and secure the pantyhose to the frame with strong tape, thumbtacks, or staples.

Paper & Paper Concoctions

Colored Paper

Now that you know the basic papermaking procedure, you can experiment with making colored paper. Be sure to refer to the Basic Paper activity (see pages 82–84) as necessary.

Here's What You Need

Newspapers
1 cup white waste paper scraps
  (See the Basic Paper supply list for
  a list of scrap material you can use.)
1 or 2 cups warm water
Large mixing bowl
Blender
Coloring item (choose 1):
  • 1 tablespoon liquid tempera paint
  • 10–20 drops food coloring
  • 2–3 teaspoons instant coffee crystals
  • 1 cup orange juice
  • 1 cup strong tea
  • 1 cup Veggie Dye (see pages 75–76)
  • 1 cup Flower Power Dye (see page 77)
Dishpan or baking pan
Papermaking screen (Follow step 1 of
  Basic Paper to make the screen.)
Terry cloth towel
Damp sponge

Rags and sponges
Rolling pin
Airtight container

Here's How You Make It

1. Cover your work area with a few sheets of newspaper. Tear white waste paper scraps into 1 cup of quarter-size pieces. (Be sure to remove any staples first.) Place the paper pieces in the bowl.

2. If you wish to color your paper with liquid tempera paint, food coloring, or instant coffee crystals, cover the paper pieces with 2 cups of warm water. If you wish to color your paper with orange juice, tea, Veggie Dye, or Flower Power Dye, cover the paper pieces with 1 cup of warm water.

3. Let the paper pieces soak for about 1 hour.

4. Ask a grownup to help you place the paper pieces and the warm water in a blender. Follow step 4 of Basic Paper to fill the blender.

Grownup Help

Add the coloring item of your choice to the blender.

5. Follow steps 5–14 of Basic Paper to make a finished sheet of colored paper.

6. You will have enough leftover pulp to make several sheets of colored paper. Repeat steps 6–14 of Basic Paper for each sheet you wish to make.

Here's How You Use It

Use your colored paper to make artwork and crafts, such as note cards, greeting cards, gift tags, bookmarks, thank-you notes, and more.

Here's How You Store It

Store the pulp in an airtight container in the fridge for up to 4 days.

Variations

● Instead of adding color to white pulp material, use colored construction paper, gift bags, fliers, or junk mail as your pulp material and follow the instructions to make Basic Paper.

● For a fun effect, stop the blender before it completely blends all the paper scraps. Some of the scraps will be larger than others, and the larger pieces will show up as splotches of color on your finished sheet of paper.

Party Paper

With flecks of shiny color, you can make unique and spectacular paper for party invitations, birthday cards, and other special artwork. Be sure to refer to the Basic Paper activity (see pages 82–84) as necessary.

Here's What You Need

Newspapers
1 cup waste paper scraps (See the Basic Paper supply list for a list of scrap material you can use.)
2 cups warm water
Large mixing bowl
Blender
Small handful of confetti or glitter
Mixing spoon
Dishpan or baking pan
Papermaking screen (Follow step 1 of Basic Paper to make the screen.)
Terry cloth towel
Damp sponge
Rags and sponges
Rolling pin
Airtight container

Here's How You Make It

1. Follow steps 2–5 of Basic Paper to make paper pulp.

2. Add the confetti or glitter to the blender and use a mixing spoon to stir them into the paper pulp material.

3. Follow steps 6–14 of Basic Paper to make a finished sheet of party paper.

4. You will have enough leftover pulp to make several sheets of party paper. Repeat steps 6–14 of Basic Paper for each sheet you wish to make.

Here's How You Use It

Use your party paper to make artwork and crafts, such as note cards, birthday cards, gift tags, invitations, thank-you notes, and more.

Here's How You Store It

Store the pulp in an airtight container in the fridge for up to 4 days.

Scented Paper

Add your own trademark scent to your paper by mixing spices, a few drops of your favorite perfume, or any other sweet-smelling items into the paper pulp. Be sure to refer to the Basic Paper activity (see pages 82–84) as necessary.

Here's What You Need

Newspapers
1 cup waste paper scraps (See the Basic Paper supply list for a list of scrap material you can use.)
2 cups warm water
Large mixing bowl
Blender
Scented item (choose 1):
- 1 teaspoon ground spices
- 1 teaspoon cocoa powder
- 1 teaspoon flavor extract
- ½ teaspoon perfume

Dishpan or baking pan
Papermaking screen (Follow step 1 of Basic Paper to make the screen.)
Terry cloth towel
Damp sponge
Rags and sponges
Rolling pin
Airtight container

Here's How You Make It

1. Follow steps 2–4 of Basic Paper to make paper pulp.

2. Ask a grownup to help you add one of the scented items to the blender.

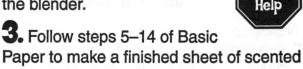

3. Follow steps 5–14 of Basic Paper to make a finished sheet of scented paper.

4. You will have enough leftover pulp to make several sheets of scented paper. Repeat steps 6–14 of Basic Paper for each sheet you wish to make.

Here's How You Use It

Use your scented paper to make sweet-smelling artwork and crafts, such as note cards, greeting cards, gift tags, bookmarks, thank-you notes, and more.

Here's How You Store It

Store the pulp in an airtight container in the fridge for up to 4 days.

Nature Paper

Here's a simple way to make sheets of paper with flower petals, grass, chopped leaves, and whatever else nature has to offer. Be sure to refer to the Basic Paper activity (see pages 82–84) as necessary.

Here's What You Need

Newspapers
1 cup waste paper scraps (See the Basic Paper supply list for a list of scrap material you can use.)
2 cups warm water
Large mixing bowl
Blender
Small handful of natural items (such as flower petals, chopped leaves, seeds, grass)
Dishpan or baking pan
Papermaking screen (Follow step 1 of Basic Paper to make the screen.)
Terry cloth towel
Damp sponge
Rags and sponges
Rolling pin
Airtight container

Here's How You Make It

1. Follow steps 2–4 of Basic Paper.

2. Ask a grownup to help you blend the paper pieces and warm water for nearly 2 minutes.

3. Add a small handful of one or more of the natural items to the blender, then blend the pulp for an additional 5 seconds. (This way, the natural items will still be visible in your finished sheet of paper.) Be sure to ask a grownup for assistance if you want to use a natural item that isn't listed above. Some natural items, like rocks or sticks, might damage your blender.

4. Follow steps 6–14 of Basic Paper to make a finished sheet of nature paper.

5. You will have enough leftover pulp to make several sheets of paper. Repeat steps 6–14 of Basic Paper for each sheet you wish to make.

Here's How You Use It

Use your nature paper to make artwork and crafts, such as note cards, greeting cards, gift tags, bookmarks, thank-you notes, and more.

Here's How You Store It

Store the pulp in an airtight container in the fridge for up to 4 days.

Variation

Press flowers between pieces of facial tissue in a heavy book, and let them dry for a couple of weeks. After you flip the paper pulp off the screen and onto the towel, gently pat the pressed flowers into the paper. Press and dry the paper as usual.

Papier-Mâché

Making papier-mâché can get really messy, but it's a lot of fun. You can make bowls, plates, piñatas, and many other fun and exciting projects with this simple concoction.

Here's What You Need

1 cup water
Medium mixing bowl
1 cup flour
Mixing spoon
Newspapers
Safety scissors
Blown-up balloon or plastic bowl or plate
Petroleum jelly or cooking spray
Tempera paint and paintbrush
Airtight container

Here's How You Make It

Pour the water in the bowl and slowly mix in the flour with the spoon. Stir the mixture until the lumps disappear.

Here's How You Use It

1. Cut several newspaper strips about 1½ inches wide and 7–8 inches long.

2. Dip the strips into the paste. Remove the excess paste by running your fingers along the strips.

3. Lightly coat a mold—such as a blown-up balloon, plastic bowl, or plastic plate—with petroleum jelly or cooking spray. Layer the newspaper strips over the mold. Be sure to overlap or crisscross the strips for extra strength.

4. Smooth out the wrinkles. If your mold is a bowl or plate, trim the excess newspaper around the edges.

5. Add a second and third layer of newspaper strips. Then let your project air-dry overnight. After it's dry, you may want to add more layers of newspaper strips and paste to reach the desired thickness for your project.

6. When the papier-mâché has hardened, gently remove the creation from the mold. If your mold is a balloon, pop and discard it.

7. Paint and decorate your creation.

Here's How You Store It

Store the papier-mâché paste in an airtight container in the fridge for up to 1 week.

Tip

Some papier-mâché creations may take several days to dry, depending on how many layers of newspaper strips you have used. If you want your project to dry faster, place it about 1 foot away from a heat vent or outside on a warm, sunny day.

Crafty Idea

Here's how to make a papier-mâché piñata:

1. Lightly coat a blown-up balloon with petroleum jelly or cooking spray.

2. Cover the balloon with 2–3 layers of newspaper strips soaked in papier-mâché paste, but leave an opening at the top where the balloon is tied.

3. Let the project air-dry overnight.

4. When the papier-mâché has hardened, pop and discard the balloon.

5. Fill your papier-mâché piñata with wrapped candies and small toys.

6. Cover the opening with masking tape, then paint and decorate the piñata.

Paper Pulp Dough

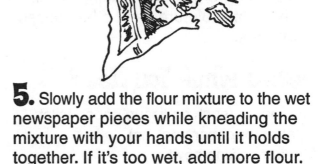

This paper pulp dough is similar to papier-mâché. It's ideal for sculpting and molding large projects, such as bowls and other 3-D works of art.

Here's What You Need

Newspaper
2 medium mixing bowls
Warm water
¼ cup flour
¼ cup water
Mixing spoon
Petroleum jelly and candy mold, cookie cutter, bottle, or milk carton (optional)
Airtight container

Here's How You Make It

1. Tear the newspaper into quarter-size pieces until you have 2 cups of packed newspaper pieces.

2. Soak the newspaper pieces in a bowl of warm water for about 1 hour.

3. Drain the water from the bowl and squeeze the excess water from the newspaper pieces.

4. In the other bowl, mix the flour and water with the spoon.

5. Slowly add the flour mixture to the wet newspaper pieces while kneading the mixture with your hands until it holds together. If it's too wet, add more flour.

Here's How You Use It

1. Mold the paper pulp dough into a 3-D sculpture. Or if you want, use your fingers to lightly coat a candy mold, cookie cutter, bottle, or milk carton with petroleum jelly, then press the dough into the candy mold or cookie cutter or over the bottle or milk carton.

2. Set your artwork aside to air-dry for 2–3 days until it's hard. If you've used a mold, gently remove the creation from the mold.

Here's How You Store It

Store the dough in an airtight container in the fridge for up to 1 week.

Fine Paper Clay

Tissue paper, toilet paper, and other fine paper are great for making small, lightweight sculptures and other pieces of artwork.

Here's What You Need

Fine paper (such as tissue paper, toilet paper, or paper napkins)
Medium mixing bowl
Warm water
4–5 tablespoons white glue (such as Elmer's School Glue)
Mixing spoon
Candy mold or cookie cutter and petroleum jelly (optional)
Tempera paint and paintbrush (optional)
Elmer's School Glue (optional)
Airtight container

Here's How You Make It

1. Tear the fine paper into quarter-size pieces until you have 2 cups of packed paper pieces.

2. Soak the paper pieces in a bowl of warm water for about 1 hour.

3. Drain the water from the bowl and squeeze the excess water from the paper pieces.

4. Add the glue 1 tablespoon at a time to the wet paper pieces while kneading the mixture with your hands until it feels like clay and sticks together.

Here's How You Use It

1. Mold the clay into a 3-D sculpture. Or if you want, use your fingers to coat a candy mold or cookie cutter with petroleum jelly, then press the dough into the candy mold or cookie cutter.

2. Set your creation aside to air-dry for 3–4 days until it's hard. If you've used a mold, gently remove the creation from the mold.

3. If you want, you can paint your artwork when it's dry and coat it with a layer of Elmer's School Glue.

Here's How You Store It

Store the clay in an airtight container in the fridge for up to 1 week.

Crafty Idea

Here's how to make beads for a necklace or bracelet:

1. Roll the clay into small balls. Poke a drinking straw through the center of each bead to make a hole.

2. Let the beads air-dry until they're hard.

3. Glue 2 or 3 layers of thin tissue paper over the beads with Elmer's School Glue, or paint the beads with acrylic or liquid tempera paint.

4. When the glue or paint has dried, thread the beads onto string to make a necklace or bracelet.

Fantastic Plastic

This "plastic" is a lot of fun to work with. Color it to look like stained glass, and cut it into many different shapes to make sun catchers and other fun artwork.

Here's What You Need

⅓ cup boiling water
2 tablespoons unflavored gelatin mix
Small mixing bowl
Fork
5–10 drops food coloring (optional)
Spoon
Large plastic margarine container
Dull knife
Cookie cutter or safety scissors
Drinking straw and thread or string
  (optional)
Wax paper

Here's How You Make It

1. Ask a grownup to help you mix the boiling water and gelatin mix in the bowl, stirring the mixture briskly with a fork until the gelatin mix dissolves. If you want colored plastic, add the food coloring to

Grownup Help

the boiling water before you combine the water with the gelatin mix. To make the plastic softer, add more water to the gelatin mix. To make it harder, add less water.

2. Use the spoon to scoop out any lumps or pop any bubbles in the mixture.

3. Pour the mixture into the margarine container.

4. Let the plastic air-dry overnight at room temperature. Do not cover it.

5. The next day, carefully remove the plastic from the margarine container using a dull knife.

Here's How You Use It

1. Cut a shape from your plastic with a cookie cutter or safety scissors. If you want to hang your creation, use a drinking straw to poke a hole at the top of the creation. When the plastic has hardened, loop a string or ribbon through the hole and tie the ends together.

Variation

To give your plastic extra sparkle, stir ¼ teaspoon of glitter or ½ teaspoon of metallic confetti into the mixture immediately after you pour it into the margarine container.

2. Set the creation aside to further harden on a sheet of wax paper. This should take anywhere from 3 days to 1 week.

Here's How You Store It

This mixture should be used up immediately after you make it. It does not store well. Put any leftover mixture in a plastic bag, then toss the bag into the garbage.

Bathtub Soap Jelly

This colorful, jellylike concoction is perfect for making soap creations you can play with in the bathtub. You can even wash yourself with this wiggly, jiggly stuff!

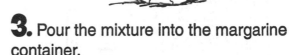

Here's What You Need

3 tablespoons hot water
3 tablespoons unflavored gelatin mix
Small mixing bowl
Fork
15–20 drops food coloring
⅛ cup liquid bubble bath
Large plastic margarine container
Wax paper
Cookie cutter or safety scissors
Plate and plastic wrap

Here's How You Make It

1. Ask a grownup to help you combine the hot water and gelatin mix in the bowl. Stir the mixture briskly with a fork until the gelatin mix dissolves.

Grownup Help

2. Immediately stir in the food coloring and the bubble bath.

3. Pour the mixture into the margarine container.

4. Refrigerate the mixture for about 1 hour.

Here's How You Use It

When the jelly is hard, remove it from the container, and lay it on a sheet of wax paper. Use a cookie cutter or safety scissors to cut shapes from the jelly.

Here's How You Store It

Store your jelly creations and any unused jelly in the fridge on a plate covered with plastic wrap for up to 5 days.

Crafty Idea

Make bathtub jewels and gemstones by cutting the jelly into diamonds, ovals, and other jewel shapes with a dull knife or safety scissors.

Crafty Jewels & Gemstones

Add sparkle to any craft project with these beautiful imitation jewels and gemstones. They're perfect for making all sorts of crafts sparkle and shine.

Here's What You Need

- 1 tablespoon Epsom salts
- 1 tablespoon boiling water
- Small glass jar
- Mixing spoon
- 5–10 drops food coloring (optional)
- Fork
- Paper towel
- Paintbrush
- Clear-drying glue (such as Elmer's School Glue)
- Ziploc bag

Here's How You Make It

1. Ask a grownup to help you mix the Epsom salts and the boiling water in the jar with the spoon. Add the food coloring if you want to make colored crystals. Stir the mixture a few times until most of the salts dissolve.

Grownup Help

2. Set the jar in a place where it won't be disturbed at room temperature. Do not cover it.

3. Beautiful crystals will grow in about 1 week. Gently scrape the crystals from the jar with a fork, and lay them on a paper towel to dry.

Here's How You Use It

Use a paintbrush to spread clear-drying glue on your artwork. Sprinkle the crystals on the glue to give your artwork a twinkling effect.

Here's How You Store It

Store the crystals for up to 1 year in a Ziploc bag at room temperature.

Crafty Idea

To make a beautiful sparkling pendant necklace, fill a clear glass or plastic necklace pendant with the crystals. Thread the pendant onto string or yarn to make a necklace.

Totally Awesome Rubber

With this totally awesome concoction, you can make a creepy rubber hand, spider, or worm. Use your imagination to create all sorts of rubber toys!

Here's What You Need

Small saucepan
3½ tablespoons unflavored gelatin mix
2 tablespoons liquid glycerin
Mixing spoon
1 tablespoon water
3–5 drops food coloring (optional)
Oven mitt
Metal or plastic molds
Plastic bag

Here's How You Make It

1. In the saucepan, combine the gelatin mix and glycerin with the spoon.

2. Add the water and stir. If you want colored rubber, add the food coloring to the water before you mix the water with the other ingredients.

3. Ask a grownup to help you place the saucepan on a stove burner and heat the mixture on medium-low, stirring the mixture constantly, until it turns into a liquid.

Grownup Help

4. Ask the grownup to help you use an oven mitt to remove the saucepan from the heat.

Here's How You Use It

1. Ask the grownup to help you pour the mixture into a metal or plastic mold, such as an insect-shaped mold, candy mold, or gelatin mold.

2. Let the rubber mixture set for 45 minutes to 1 hour.

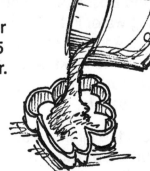

3. When the rubber is set, scoop it out of the mold using your fingers or the spoon.

Here's How You Store It

This mixture should be used up immediately after you make it. It does not store well. Put any leftover mixture in a plastic bag, then toss the bag into the garbage.

Tip

Can't find a mold? Make your own mold out of plaster. Follow the package instructions to make plaster of Paris, then pour the plaster into an empty plastic margarine container. When the plaster begins to set (about 20–25 minutes), press a toy, your hand or foot, or any object of your choice into the plaster. Remove the object from the plaster. When the plaster has completely hardened, rub some petroleum jelly onto the impression. Pour your rubber mixture into the mold and let it harden for 45 minutes to 1 hour. When the rubber is set, scoop it out of the mold using your fingers or the spoon.

Sticky Goo

This stuff feels strange when you squish it through your fingers. It's a little tricky, kinda sticky, and really icky!

Here's What You Need

Large saucepan
½ cup salt
¼ cup warm water
10–15 drops food coloring
Mixing spoon
Oven mitt
1 cup cornstarch
¼ cup cold water
Paper
Ziploc bag and safety scissors (optional)
Airtight container

Here's How You Make It

1. In the saucepan, mix the salt, warm water, and food coloring with the spoon.

2. Ask a grownup to help you place the saucepan on a stove burner and bring the mixture to a boil. Stir the mixture constantly for about 1 minute.

3. Ask the grownup to help you use an oven mitt to remove the saucepan from the heat.

4. Let the mixture cool for 5 minutes, stirring it occasionally.

5. Stir in the cornstarch and cold water while the mixture is still warm.

6. When the mixture is cool enough to handle, mix it with your hands.

Here's How You Use It

1. Grab a handful of the goo and drizzle it onto a sheet of paper in different patterns, shapes, and designs. Or if you want, pour the goo into a Ziploc bag that has one of its bottom corners cut off, seal the bag, and squeeze the goo out onto the paper.

2. Set your artwork aside to harden.

Here's How You Store It

Store the goo in an airtight container at room temperature for up to 2 days.

Flubber Rubber

With this rubbery concoction, you can make spiders, bugs, blob monsters, and more. Like, totally *yuck!*

Here's What You Need

2 small mixing bowls
2 tablespoons white glue (such as Elmer's School Glue)
3–5 drops food coloring
Mixing spoon
1 teaspoon cornstarch
1 package unflavored gelatin mix
2 tablespoons hot water
Fork
Mold
Wax paper
Googly eyes, small buttons, or pipe cleaners (optional)
Airtight container or Ziploc bag
Plastic bag

Here's How You Make It

1. In one bowl, mix the glue and the food coloring with the spoon. Stir in the cornstarch.

2. Ask a grownup to help you combine the gelatin mix and the hot water in the other bowl, stirring the mixture briskly with a fork until the gelatin mix completely dissolves.

> Grownup Help

3. Let the gelatin mixture cool for 1 minute, then pour it into the glue mixture.

4. Stir the two mixtures together with the spoon for about 3 minutes until the new mixture is thick and gummy.

Here's How You Use It

1. To make a rubbery toy, pour the mixture into a mold. If you want to make a blob monster, spoon a blob of the mixture onto a sheet of wax paper, and decorate it with googly eyes, small buttons, or pipe cleaners.

2. Place the mold or the blob monster in the freezer to firm for about 10 minutes.

3. Remove the mold or blob monster from the freezer. (Carefully remove the creation from the mold at this time.) Place the creation on a sheet of wax paper.

4. Let your creation air-dry for 2–3 days until it's hard. If you let your creation air-dry too long, it will become like hard plastic.

Here's How You Store It

Store your creation for several months in an airtight container or Ziploc bag at room temperature. Put any leftover rubber mixture in a plastic bag, then toss the bag into the garbage.

Imitation Sand

This imitation sand adds interesting texture and a sprinkling of color to your artwork. You can also use it to make bright, colorful terrarium art.

Here's What You Need

½ cup salt
½ cup cornmeal
Large Ziploc bag
1–1½ tablespoons
   liquid tempera
   paint (a bright
   color works best)

Paper towel
White glue (such as
   Elmer's School
   Glue)
Heavy paper

Here's How You Make It

1. Pour the salt and cornmeal into the Ziploc bag.

2. Zip the bag shut and shake it a few times to mix the ingredients.

3. Add the liquid tempera paint, close the bag, and shake it vigorously. The paint should coat the imitation sand mixture thoroughly without making it too wet.

4. Pour the mixture onto a paper towel to dry.

Here's How You Use It

1. Draw designs or write your name by squeezing glue onto a sheet of heavy paper.

2. Sprinkle the imitation sand onto the wet glue and shake off the excess.

Here's How You Store It

Store the imitation sand in the Ziploc bag at room temperature for up to 1 year.

Crafty Idea

To make an imitation-sand terrarium, make up several bags of imitation sand, using a different color of paint for each batch. Pour or spoon the sand into a glass jar, using a different color for each layer. Use a pencil or knitting needle to poke into the sand to form hills and valleys. When finished, seal the lid on the jar with glue.

Forever Flowers

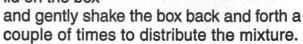

If you like to make crafts using fresh flowers, here's a concoction that will keep your flowers summer fresh forever!

Here's What You Need

Safety scissors
Fresh flowers
Mixing bowl
2 cups borax
4 cups cornmeal

Mixing spoon
Shoebox with lid
White glue (such as Elmer's School Glue)
Airtight container

Here's How You Make It

1. Trim each flower stem so there's about 1 inch of stem left below the flower.

2. In the bowl, thoroughly mix the borax and cornmeal with the spoon.

3. Cover the bottom of the shoebox with ½–¾ inch of the mixture.

4. Lay the flowers facedown in the mixture, and spread the petals and leaves a bit.

5. Cover the flowers with an additional ¾–1 inch of the mixture.

6. Place the lid on the box and gently shake the box back and forth a couple of times to distribute the mixture.

7. Set the box in a place where it will be undisturbed for about 1 month at room temperature. Then carefully remove the flowers from the mixture.

Here's How You Use It

Glue the preserved flowers onto your artwork. Or use the flowers to make a corsage or wreath.

Here's How You Store It

Store the mixture in an airtight container at room temperature for several months.

Tip Because it takes about 1 month to preserve the flowers, be sure to plan this activity well in advance of your final craft project.

3-D Sand

When this sandy concoction dries, it'll be hard and puffy. You can use it to outline your artwork or draw pictures, letters, and other 3-D designs.

Here's What You Need

Mixing bowl
⅓ cup flour
⅓ cup fine, dry sandbox sand or beach
  sand
⅓ cup water
Mixing spoon
½ teaspoon food coloring or 2 tablespoons
  powdered tempera paint (optional)
Ziploc bag and safety scissors or plastic
  squeeze bottle
Heavy construction paper, paper plate,
  or cardboard
Airtight container or Ziploc bag

Here's How You Make It

1. In the bowl, mix the flour, sand, and water with the spoon. If you want colored 3-D sand, add the food coloring or powdered tempera paint to the water before you mix the water with the other ingredients.

2. Pour the mixture into a Ziploc bag that has the tip of one of its bottom corners cut off, then seal the bag. Or pour the mixture into a plastic squeeze bottle.

Here's How You Use It

1. Squeeze the mixture onto heavy construction paper, a paper plate, or cardboard.

2. Set your artwork aside to dry overnight.

Here's How You Store It

Store the sand mixture in an airtight container or Ziploc bag at room temperature for up to 1 week.

Puffy Mud

This puffy concoction starts out wet and slimy, then it turns soft and fluffy the more you squish it. Super soft, super cool, super clean!

Here's What You Need

Single-size roll of two-ply toilet paper
2 large mixing bowls
3.1-ounce bar of Ivory soap
Cheese grater
2½ cups hot water
Mixing spoon
1 cup powdered
   laundry detergent
   (optional)
Large tray or baking sheet
Airtight container

Here's How You Make It

1. Tear the entire roll of toilet paper into tiny pieces, and place them in one bowl.

2. Grate the bar of soap using the cheese grater, and place the shavings in the other bowl.

3. Add the hot water to the soap shavings and stir them with the spoon.

4. Add the soap shaving mixture to the toilet paper pieces.

5. Squish the mixture between your fingers until it's like soft, fluffy mashed potatoes. If the mixture gets too soupy, add more toilet paper pieces.

6. If you want to make a permanent creation, add the detergent.

Here's How You Use It

1. Place the mixture on a large tray or baking sheet and mold it into any shape you wish. The more you squish it, the puffier and softer it will get.

2. If you want to make your creation permanent, let it air-dry overnight. (A large sculpture may take several days to harden.)

Here's How You Store It

Store the mixture in an airtight container in the fridge for up to 1 week.

Sculpting Putty

If you like to mold, squish, and smoosh stuff together, here's a fun, moldable putty you can make into all sorts of different shapes.

Here's What You Need

Two 1-by-1-inch cubes beeswax
Cheese grater
Tin can
Saucepan
Water
4 crayons
Popsicle stick
Oven mitt
Paper cup or plastic container
1 tablespoon petroleum jelly
1 teaspoon baby oil or vegetable oil
Plate (optional)
Ziploc bag

Here's How You Make It

1. Grate the beeswax using the smallest hole on your cheese grater until you have 2 tablespoons of packed shavings.

2. Put the beeswax shavings in a tin can, then place the can in a saucepan filled with 1–2 inches of water.

3. Ask a grownup to help you place the saucepan on a stove burner and simmer the water on medium-low until the beeswax melts.

4. Remove the labels from the crayons. Ask the grownup to help you add the crayons to the melted beeswax, stirring the mixture occasionally with a Popsicle stick.

5. When the crayons completely melt, ask the grownup to help you use an oven mitt to remove the saucepan from the heat, then remove the can from the saucepan.

6. Ask the grownup to help you pour the mixture into a paper cup or plastic container.

7. Immediately stir in the petroleum jelly and baby oil or vegetable oil.

8. Set the mixture aside to cool for 25–30 minutes, stirring it occasionally.

9. When the mixture has cooled and no longer feels sticky, knead it with your hands until it's smooth.

Here's How You Use It

1. Mold the putty into any shape you wish.

2. If you want to make your creation permanent, place it on a plate in the fridge for 20 minutes.

Here's How You Store It

Store the putty in a Ziploc bag at room temperature for several months.

Tutti-Frutti Lip-Gloss

Choose your favorite fruity Jell-O flavor to make this lip-smackin' lip-gloss!

Here's What You Need

Small microwave-safe mixing bowl
1½ teaspoons pink or red Jell-O mix
1 teaspoon hot water
Mixing spoon
1 tablespoon petroleum jelly
Oven mitt
½ teaspoon pink or red Kool-Aid mix
Small plastic container with lid
Toothpick (optional)

Here's How You Make It

1. In the bowl, combine the Jell-O mix with the hot water with the spoon. Stir until the Jell-O mix completely dissolves.

2. Add the petroleum jelly and stir the mixture.

3. Ask a grownup to help you microwave the mixture for 15 seconds on high.

4. Holding the bowl with an oven mitt, stir the mixture well, then set it aside to cool for about 5 minutes.

5. Stir in the Kool-Aid mix.

6. Pour the mixture into a small plastic container.

Here's How You Use It

Apply the lip-gloss to your lips with your fingers. You may need to mix it once or twice with a toothpick first.

Here's How You Store It

Store the lip-gloss in the plastic container at room temperature for up to 2 weeks.

Honeybee Lip Balm

This sweet-as-honey lip balm protects dry lips—and smiles, too!

Here's What You Need

One 1-by-1-inch cube beeswax
Cheese grater
Tin can
Small saucepan
Water
¼ piece red or pink crayon (optional)
2 tablespoons olive oil
Mixing spoon
Oven mitt
1½ teaspoons honey
¼ teaspoon vanilla extract
Small plastic container with lid

Here's How You Make It

1. Grate the beeswax using the smallest hole on your cheese grater until you have 1 tablespoon of packed shavings.

2. Put the beeswax shavings in a tin can, then place the can in a saucepan filled with 1–2 inches of water. If you want colored lip balm, add the crayon piece to the tin can.

3. Ask a grownup to help you place the saucepan on a stove burner and simmer the water on low until the beeswax completely melts.

Grownup Help

4. Stir the olive oil into the melted beeswax with the spoon.

5. Ask the grownup to help you use an oven mitt to remove the saucepan from the heat, then remove the can from the saucepan.

6. Stir the honey and vanilla extract into the beeswax.

7. Ask the grownup to help you pour the mixture into a small plastic container.

8. To mix the honey evenly throughout the container, stir the mixture after it cools but before it completely hardens.

9. Refrigerate the lip balm for about 30 minutes.

Here's How You Use It

Apply the lip balm to your lips with your fingers.

Here's How You Store It

Store the lip balm in the plastic container at room temperature for up to 1 year.

Halloween Face Putty

For a fabulous made-up face for Halloween, try this awesome face putty instead of a mask. It's rich and smooth, and it'll stay on all day—even when you bob for apples!

Here's What You Need

2 crayons
Tin can
Saucepan
Water
Oven mitt
Paper cup
1 tablespoon
  petroleum jelly

Popsicle stick
Small microwave-safe
  plastic container
  with lid
Sponge or cotton
  swab

Here's How You Make It

1. Remove the labels from the crayons.

2. Put the crayons in a tin can, then place the can in a saucepan filled with 1–2 inches of water.

3. Ask a grownup to help you place the saucepan on a stove burner and simmer the water on medium-low until the crayons melt.

4. Ask the grownup to help you use the oven mitt to remove the saucepan from the heat, then remove the can from the saucepan.

5. Ask the grownup to help you pour the melted crayon into a paper cup.

6. Immediately stir in the petroleum jelly with a Popsicle stick. Continue stirring until the petroleum jelly completely melts.

7. Let the mixture cool for about 10 minutes and then stir it again.

8. Use the Popsicle stick to scoop the mixture into a small plastic container. Let it cool and harden into a putty.

Here's How You Use It

1. To test for an allergic reaction, apply a small amount of the putty to the inside of your wrist the night before you apply it to your face. Store the rest of the putty overnight.

2. If your skin doesn't react to the putty, wash and dry your skin where you will apply the putty.

3. Apply the putty to your face with your fingers, a sponge, or a cotton swab. Be sure to keep the putty out of your eyes.

4. When it's time to clean up, wash off the face putty with soap and water.

Here's How You Store It

Store the face putty in the plastic container at room temperature for up to 2 weeks.

Tip Ask a grownup to help you microwave the putty for a few seconds if it gets too hard and becomes difficult to spread.

Crafty Ideas With some imagination, you can create all kinds of fabulous effects!

● **Bruises:** Apply some blue or purple face putty wherever you want a bruise to appear. Add a very small amount of yellow face putty to create an old bruise or a small amount of red face putty to create a new bruise. For a real shiner, apply a thin coat of petroleum jelly on top of the putty.

● **Blackened-Out Teeth:** To blacken out your teeth for a hillbilly or hockey player costume, first dry your teeth with a facial tissue, then color them with black face putty.

Super Shine Lip-Gloss

Give your lips a super shine with this fabulous liquid lip-gloss. It goes on clear and glossy.

Here's What You Need

Paper cup
1 teaspoon
  petroleum jelly
1 teaspoon
  liquid glycerin
1 teaspoon baby oil
  or mineral oil
Mixing spoon

Oven mitt
Small plastic
  container with lid
Toothpick
3–5 drops flavor
  extract
Cotton swab

Here's How You Make It

1. In a paper cup, mix the petroleum jelly, glycerin, and baby oil or mineral oil with the spoon.

2. Ask a grownup to help you microwave the mixture on high for about 30 seconds.

Grownup Help

3. Ask the grownup to help you use an oven mitt to remove the paper cup from the microwave.

4. Stir the mixture well, then carefully pour it into a small plastic container.

5. Let your lip-gloss cool in the container.

6. Use a toothpick to stir in the flavor extract.

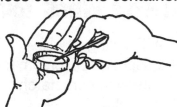

Here's How You Use It

Apply the lip-gloss to your lips with a cotton swab or your fingers. You may need to stir it with a toothpick first.

Here's How You Store It

Store the lip-gloss in the plastic container at room temperature for up to 1 month.

Variation

For extra sparkle, use a toothpick to stir a couple of pinches of ultrafine glitter into the lip-gloss before it cools in the container.

Clown Face Paint

This simple recipe makes a great face paint for clown or Halloween costumes, and it's easy to wash off with soap and water.

Here's What You Need

Small mixing bowl
1 teaspoon cold cream (such as Noxzema)
1 teaspoon cornstarch
Toothpick
5–6 drops food coloring
Sponge, cotton swab, or small paintbrush
Small plastic container with lid

Here's How You Make It

1. In the bowl, mix the cold cream and the cornstarch with a toothpick until the mixture is creamy.

2. Add the food coloring to make a dark, rich color.

Here's How You Use It

1. To test for an allergic reaction, apply a small amount of the paint to the inside of your wrist the night before you apply it to your face. Store the rest of the paint overnight.

2. If your skin doesn't react to the face paint, wash and dry your skin where you will apply the face paint.

3. Apply the face paint with your fingers, a sponge, a cotton swab, or a small paintbrush. Be careful not to get the mixture in your eyes because it may make them sting.

Here's How You Store It

Store the face paint in a small plastic container at room temperature for up to 1 week.

Luscious Lipstick

With this creative concoction, you can make rich, creamy, luscious lipstick. Perfect for dress-up play, Halloween costumes, and sleepover fun.

Here's What You Need

1 crayon
Tin can
Saucepan
Water
Oven mitt
1 teaspoon baby oil
Popsicle stick
Small plastic container with lid
Cotton swab

Here's How You Make It

1. Remove the label from your crayon.

2. Put the crayon in a tin can, then place the can in a saucepan filled with 1–2 inches of water.

3. Ask a grownup to help you place the saucepan on a stove burner and simmer the water on medium-low until the crayon melts.

Grownup Help

4. Ask the grownup to help you use the oven mitt to remove the saucepan from the heat, then remove the can from the saucepan.

5. Immediately stir the baby oil into the melted crayon, using a Popsicle stick.

6. Ask the grownup to help you pour the mixture into a small plastic container.

7. Let the lipstick cool.

Here's How You Use It

Apply the lipstick to your lips with a cotton swab or your fingers.

Here's How You Store It

Store the lipstick in the plastic container at room temperature for several months.

Variations

● To make your lipstick glossier, add an additional ¼–½ teaspoon of baby oil.

● To make shimmering lipstick, add a couple pinches of ultrafine glitter after you stir in the baby oil.

● Instead of using one crayon to make your lipstick, mix pieces of different crayons to create your perfect personalized shade. Here are some cool color combos to try:

- **Marvelous Mauve:** ¾ pink crayon + ¼ light blue crayon
- **Dusty Rose:** ¾ pink crayon + ¼ gray crayon
- **Perfect Peach:** ½ orange crayon + ½ white crayon
- **Passionate Pink:** ½ red crayon + ½ white crayon

Body Art Concoctions & Cosmetics

Tattoo Paint

Here's a fun and creative way to make tattoo paint—but don't worry, it washes off with soap and water! Decorate your body with whatever creative designs you can dream up.

Here's What You Need

1 crayon
Tin can
Saucepan
Water
2 teaspoons petroleum jelly
Oven mitt
Paper cup
Mixing spoon
½ teaspoon cold cream (such as Noxzema)
Small plastic container with lid
Small paintbrush, toothpick, or cotton swab
Soap and water

Here's How You Make It

1. Remove the label from your crayon.

2. Put the crayon in a tin can, then place the can in a saucepan filled with 1–2 inches of water.

3. Ask a grownup to help you place the saucepan on a stove burner and simmer the water on medium-low until the crayon melts.

Grownup Help

4. Add the petroleum jelly and continue heating the mixture for 1 minute, stirring frequently.

5. Ask the grownup to help you use an oven mitt to remove the saucepan from the heat, then remove the can from the saucepan.

6. Ask the grownup to help you pour the mixture into a paper cup.

7. Let the mixture cool for about 1 minute, then use the spoon to stir in the cold cream.

8. Spoon the mixture out of the paper cup and into a small plastic container.

Here's How You Use It

1. To test for an allergic reaction, apply a small amount of the tattoo paint to the inside of your wrist the night before you apply it to your face or body. Store the rest of the paint overnight.

2. If your skin doesn't react to the tattoo paint, wash and dry your skin where you want to apply the tattoo paint.

3. Use a small paintbrush, toothpick, cotton swab, or your fingers to draw a tattoo design on your face or body. Keep the paint out of your eyes.

4. When it's time to clean up, remove the paint with soap and water.

Here's How You Store It

Store the tattoo paint in the plastic container at room temperature for up to 2 weeks.

Lavish Lipslick

Lipslick has the color of a lipstick and the shine of a lip-gloss. Use it to color your lips or cheeks for dress-up or other imaginative play. You'll look *mahvelous!*

Here's What You Need

1 pink or red crayon
Tin can
Saucepan
Water
Oven mitt
Paper cup
1 tablespoon petroleum jelly
Popsicle stick
3–5 drops flavor extract
Mixing spoon
Cotton swab
Small plastic container with lid

Here's How You Make It

1. Remove the label from your crayon.

2. Put the crayon in a tin can, then place the can in a saucepan filled with 1–2 inches of water.

3. Ask a grownup to help you place the saucepan on a stove burner and simmer the water on medium-low until the crayon melts.

Grownup Help

4. Ask the grownup to help you use an oven mitt to remove the saucepan from the heat, then remove the can from the saucepan.

5. Ask the grownup to help you pour the melted crayon into a paper cup.

6. Immediately stir in the petroleum jelly using a Popsicle stick.

7. Let the mixture cool slightly, then stir in the flavor extract.

8. Spoon your lipslick out of the paper cup and into a small plastic container.

Here's How You Use It

Apply the lipslick to your lips with a cotton swab or your fingers.

Here's How You Store It

Store the lipslick in the plastic container at room temperature for several months.

Fake Blood

This oozing, dripping "blood" looks just like the real thing! If your parents run for the first-aid kit after they catch a glimpse of you, you've done a great job!

Here's What You Need

Small mixing bowl
½ teaspoon cocoa powder
1½ teaspoons hot water
Mixing spoon
2 tablespoons corn syrup
15–20 drops red food coloring
Eyedropper or spoon
Airtight container

Here's How You Make It

1. In the bowl, mix the cocoa powder and hot water with the spoon.

2. Add the corn syrup and stir well.

3. Mix in the food coloring.

Here's How You Use It

1. To test for an allergic reaction, apply a small amount of the fake blood to the inside of your wrist the night before you apply it to your face or body. Store the rest of the fake blood overnight.

2. If your skin doesn't react to the fake blood, wash and dry your skin where you want to apply the fake blood.

3. Use an eyedropper or a spoon to drip the fake blood from the corners of your mouth, onto a costume bandage, or onto whatever you want to look bloody. Keep fake blood away from clothing, because it may stain.

Here's How You Store It

Store the fake blood in an airtight container in the fridge for up to 1 week.

Creepy Skin

Use this creepy concoction to create a horrifying flesh wound for a frightful Halloween costume. Creep out your parents. Freak out your friends. Astonish the neighbors. The fun never ends!

Here's What You Need

Small mixing bowl
3 tablespoons oatmeal or bread crumbs
1 tablespoon water
1 tablespoon Elmer's School Glue
1 tablespoon cornstarch
Mixing spoon
Spatula or Popsicle stick

Here's How You Make It

In the bowl, mix the oatmeal or bread crumbs, water, glue, and cornstarch with the spoon to form a thick paste.

Here's How You Use It

1. Wash and dry your skin where you want to apply the mixture.

2. Spread the mixture onto your skin using a spatula or Popsicle stick.

3. Let the mixture dry for about 15 minutes.

Here's How You Store It

This mixture must be used up immediately after you make it. It does not store well. Put any leftover mixture in a plastic bag, then toss the bag into the garbage.

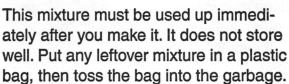

Tip Be sure to test for an allergic reaction before you make and use the concoction. Use a Popsicle stick to mix ¼ teaspoon oatmeal or bread crumbs, ¼ teaspoon water, ¼ teaspoon Elmer's School Glue, and ¼ teaspoon cornstarch in a paper cup. Apply the mixture to the inside of your wrist and let it set overnight.

Scars, Scabs, Burns, & Wrinkles

Here's a trick Hollywood makeup artists have been using for years to create realistic scars, scabs, burns, and wrinkles on skin.

Here's What You Need

Small mixing bowl
2 teaspoons unflavored gelatin mix
1 tablespoon hot water
Fork
Paintbrush
Red food coloring or Fake Blood (see page 122)
Blow dryer (optional)
Makeup (optional)

Here's How You Make It

1. In the bowl, stir the gelatin mix and hot water briskly with a fork until the gelatin mix dissolves.

2. Let the mixture cool until it becomes thick and gooey.

Here's How You Use It

1. Wash and dry your skin where you want to apply the mixture.

2. To make scars, scabs, and burns, use a paintbrush or your fingers to apply a thick layer of the mixture onto your skin. Add 1–2 drops of red food coloring or Fake Blood for an added effect. To make wrinkles, use a paintbrush or your fingers to apply an even layer of the mixture onto your skin, spreading the mixture out as much as possible. Work fast because this mixture can harden quickly.

3. Let the mixture dry for about 10 minutes, or if you're in a hurry dry it with a blow dryer on a cool setting.

4. If you wish, you can use makeup to color the scars, scabs, burns, and wrinkles.

Here's How You Store It

This mixture must be used up immediately after you make it. It does not store well. Put any leftover mixture in a plastic bag, then toss the bag into the garbage.

Tip

Be sure to test for an allergic reaction before you make and use the concoction. Use a Popsicle stick to mix ¼ teaspoon unflavored gelatin mix, ¼ teaspoon hot water, and 1 drop red food coloring (optional) in a paper cup. Apply the mixture to the inside of your wrist and let it set overnight.

Variation

To create a more natural skin tone, add ½ teaspoon of liquid foundation makeup to the hot water before you mix the water with the gelatin mix.

Mummy Paste

Apply this gruesome paste, and you'll look like a frightful mummy, a scary monster, or a creepy zombie who just stepped out of the graveyard. *Eeeeek!*

Here's What You Need

Medium mixing bowl
¼ cup salt
¾ cup water
Mixing spoon
¾ cup flour
Safety scissors
Paper towels
Blow dryer or fan (optional)
Airtight container

Here's How You Make It

1. In the bowl, mix the salt and water with the spoon.

2. Mix in the flour. Stir well to remove all lumps.

Here's How You Use It

1. To test for an allergic reaction, apply a small amount of the paste to the inside of your wrist the night before you apply it to your face or body.

2. If your skin doesn't react to the paste, wash and dry your skin where you want to apply the paste.

3. To make a zombie, monster, or mummy costume, cut or tear a paper towel into 1-by-5-inch strips and into 3-by-11-inch strips.

4. Dip the paper towel strips into the paste. Remove as much excess paste as you can by running your fingers along each paper towel strip.

5. Apply the 1-by-5-inch strips to your face, cheeks, and forehead. Wrap the 3-by-11-inch strips around your arms, legs, and hands.

6. Press the strips firmly with your hands to remove as much excess paste as you can. Let the strips dry, which can take 2–4 hours, depending on the thickness of your paper towel layers. If you're in a hurry, use a blow dryer on a cool setting or sit in front of a fan to speed up the drying.

Here's How You Store It

Store the paste in an airtight container in the fridge for up to 3–4 days.

Tip If portions of the paper towel layers begin to peel off, simply brush on a small amount of nontoxic glue (such as Elmer's School Glue) or leftover paste to soften and secure the edges.

Special Effects Rubber

To add a little extra fright to a Halloween costume, use this rubbery stuff to make warts, lumps, bumps, and boils.

Here's What You Need

Small saucepan
1 tablespoon clear, unflavored gelatin mix
2 teaspoons liquid glycerin
1 tablespoon hot water
1 tablespoon corn syrup
Mixing spoon
5–10 drops food coloring (optional)
Oven mitt
Plastic wrap
Nontoxic glue (such as Elmer's School Glue)

Here's How You Make It

1. In a saucepan, combine the gelatin mix, glycerin, hot water, and corn syrup with the spoon. If you want colored rubber, mix the food coloring with the hot water before you add the water to the other ingredients.

2. Ask a grownup to help you place the saucepan on a stove burner. Heat the mixture on medium-low, stirring constantly, until it starts to bubble.

3. Ask the grownup to help you use an oven mitt to remove the saucepan from the heat. Let the mixture cool slightly.

4. Ask the grownup to help you drip some of the mixture onto a piece of plastic wrap. Let the mixture harden for a few minutes.

5. Gently peel the hardened rubber from the plastic wrap.

Here's How You Use It

1. Wash and dry your skin where you want to apply the mixture.

2. Wet and stick the rubbery pieces onto your face, arms, or legs to make warts, moles, lumps, and boils. To apply a larger piece, spread nontoxic glue on the rubber then hold the glue-covered rubber to your skin for about 1 minute or until it begins to stick.

Here's How You Store It

This mixture must be used up immediately after you make it. It does not store well. Put any leftover mixture in a plastic bag, then toss the bag into the garbage.

Tip

Be sure to test for an allergic reaction before you make and use the concoction. Use a Popsicle stick to mix ¼ teaspoon unflavored gelatin mix, ¼ teaspoon liquid glycerin, ¼ teaspoon hot water, ¼ teaspoon corn syrup, and 1 drop food coloring (optional) in a paper cup. Apply the mixture to the inside of your wrist and let it set overnight.

Crafty Idea

Here's how you can make a third eye for a monster costume:

1. Pour the rubber mixture into an eggcup, and let it harden in the fridge for about 1 hour.

2. Scoop your eyeball out of the eggcup, and paint the eyeball with nontoxic liquid tempera paint.

3. Use nontoxic glue or special effects wax (a special substance available at costume shops and used to apply small props to skin) to glue the eyeball to your forehead.

Foaming Paste

Spread some out-of-this-world paste on your hands or arms to make your skin foam and bubble. Your friends will think you're an alien from another planet!

Here's What You Need

Small mixing bowl
1½ tablespoons baking soda
1 tablespoon corn syrup
Mixing spoon
Spatula
½ teaspoon baking soda
1–2 teaspoons white vinegar
Airtight container

Here's How You Make It

In the bowl, mix the 1½ tablespoons of baking soda and the corn syrup with the spoon until a paste forms.

Here's How You Use It

1. To test for an allergic reaction, apply a small amount of the paste on the inside of your wrist the night before you apply it to your body.

2. If your skin doesn't react to the paste, wash and dry your skin where you want to create a foam.

3. Spread the paste on your arms, legs, and body using a spatula or your fingers. Keep the mixture away from your face, eyes, and open cuts because it may make those areas sting.

4. Sprinkle the ½ teaspoon of baking soda on top of the paste and pat it gently into the paste.

5. Drip the vinegar onto the paste, and watch it foam and fizz!

Here's How You Store It

Store the paste in an airtight container in the fridge for up to 1–2 days.

Variation

To make foaming "blood," mix 1–3 drops of red food coloring with the vinegar before you drip the vinegar on the paste.

Special Effects

Swamp Gunk

Smear this totally disgusting, slimy gunk over your body to look like a creature that just crept out of a swamp.

Here's What You Need

6 tablespoons hot water
Small mixing bowl
2 tablespoons unflavored gelatin mix
Mixing spoon
5 tablespoons corn syrup
1–2 drops green food coloring (optional)
Fork

Here's How You Make It

1. Pour the hot water into the bowl. Sprinkle the gelatin mix on the water.

2. Stir the mixture once or twice with the spoon, then leave it to set and cool for 1 minute.

3. Stir the mixture a few more times, then add the corn syrup. If you want colored swamp gunk, mix the green food coloring with the corn syrup before you add it to the mixture. Stir the mixture once again.

Here's How You Use It

1. Wash and dry your skin where you want to apply the mixture.

2. Lift out the gooey, stringy gunk using a fork or your fingers. Spread the mixture on your arms, legs, or face. Keep it out of your eyes because it may make them sting.

3. Let the mixture harden for about 30 minutes.

Here's How You Store It

This mixture must be used up immediately after you make it. It does not store well. Put any leftover mixture in a plastic bag, then toss the bag into the garbage.

Tip Be sure to test for an allergic reaction before you make and use the concoction. Use a Popsicle stick to mix ¼ teaspoon hot water, ¼ teaspoon unflavored gelatin mix, ¼ teaspoon corn syrup, and 1 drop green food coloring (optional) in a paper cup. Apply the mixture to the inside of your wrist and let it set overnight.

Edible Finger Paints

Food, glorious food! Get ready for some downright messy fun with these finger-lickin' finger paints.

Here's What You Need

Plastic drop cloth or newspapers
Edible finger paints (choose 1 or more):
- ¼ cup chocolate pudding mixed with ¼ cup whipped cream or Cool Whip
- ½ cup vanilla pudding mixed with 3–4 drops food coloring
- ¼ cup corn syrup mixed with 2–3 drops food coloring
- ¼ cup chocolate syrup mixed with 5–10 drops flavor extract

Small mixing bowls
Mixing spoons
Wax paper
Airtight containers

Here's How You Make It

1. Lay a drop cloth or newspapers on the floor under your work area.

2. Mix up the edible finger paints in separate bowls with separate spoons.

Here's How You Use It

1. Wash and dry your hands.

2. Finger paint with these concoctions on a sheet of wax paper.

3. When you're done, have great fun eating your artwork!

Here's How You Store It

Store each finger paint in an airtight container in the fridge for up to 3–4 days.

Edible Play Dough

If you like peanut butter, you'll love this play dough. Not only is it fun to play with, but it's deliciously edible as well. Yummy, yummy, yummy!

Here's What You Need

Large mixing bowl
1 cup creamy peanut butter
1 cup powdered milk
⅔ cup sugar
¼ cup honey
⅔ cup shredded coconut, raisins,
  or chocolate chips
Wax paper

Here's How You Make It

1. Wash and dry your hands.

2. In the bowl, use your fingers to mix the peanut butter and the powdered milk.

3. Mix in the sugar, honey, and coconut, raisins, or chocolate chips until the mixture is well blended.

4. Work the mixture with your fingers until it's like play dough. Add more powdered milk if the dough is too sticky.

Here's How You Use It

Mold this edible dough the same way you'd mold regular play dough. Build your creation on a sheet of wax paper, then eat it!

Here's How You Store It

This dough should be used up the same day you make it. It does not store well. Put any leftover dough in a plastic bag, then toss the bag into the garbage.

Candy Clay

If you like chocolate, you'll love mixing up a batch of this sticky stuff! You can mold it as you would mold any other clay, but the best part is, you get to eat this creation afterward. Enjoy!

Here's What You Need

1½ teaspoons butter	Mixing spoon
8 ounces chocolate or 1 cup chocolate chips	Oven mitt
	¼ cup corn syrup
Medium saucepan	Airtight container
	Wax paper

Here's How You Make It

1. Place the butter and chocolate or chocolate chips in the saucepan.

2. Ask a grownup to help you place the saucepan on a stove burner and heat the mixture on medium-low. Stir the mixture frequently with the spoon until it completely melts.

3. Ask the grownup to help you use an oven mitt to remove the saucepan from the heat.

4. Ask the grownup to help you stir in the corn syrup.

5. Let the mixture cool slightly, then pour it into an airtight container.

6. Let the candy clay harden in the fridge for 45 minutes to 1 hour.

Here's How You Use It

1. Wash and dry your hands.

2. Place the candy clay on a sheet of wax paper.

3. Mold it into any shape you wish, then eat it!

Here's How You Store It

This clay must be used up the same day you make it. It does not store well. Put any leftover clay in a plastic bag, then toss the bag into the garbage.

Lick-It Stick-It Glue

Make your own tasty-to-lick, fun-to-stick stickers and stamps with this simple glue concoction.

Here's What You Need

2 teaspoons Jell-O mix
1 tablespoon boiling water
Small mixing bowl
Mixing spoon
½ teaspoon corn syrup
Small paintbrush
Paper
Artwork

Here's How You Make It

1. Ask a grownup to help you combine the Jell-O mix and the boiling water in the bowl. Stir the mixture with the spoon until the Jell-O mix dissolves.

2. Stir in the corn syrup.

3. Let the glue mixture cool slightly.

Here's How You Use It

1. Using a small paintbrush, spread the glue mixture onto a piece of paper you want to stick to your artwork.

2. Let the glue mixture dry.

3. Lick the glue and stick the paper onto your artwork.

Here's How You Store It

This glue should be used up immediately after you make it. It does not store well. Put any leftover glue in a plastic bag, then toss the bag into the garbage.

Crafty Ideas

● Cut small pictures from colorful gift-wrap, magazines, or greeting cards. Paint the glue onto the back of the picture, then lick and stick your own homemade stickers.

● Decorate a piece of paper that's the size of a postage stamp. Paint on the glue, then lick and stick the pretend stamp on a greeting card envelope.

Delicious Diamonds

Make it sparkle! Make it shine! These dazzling "diamonds" are not only beautiful to wear, but fun to eat, too.

Here's What You Need

Saucepan
1 cup water
2½ cups sugar
Wooden or metal spoon
Oven mitt
1 or 2 clear glass jars
Safety scissors

Heavy construction paper or cardboard
Bamboo skewer
Fork
Paper towel
Corn syrup or Tasty Glue (see page 140)
Airtight container
Plastic bag

Here's How You Make It

1. Ask a grownup to help you with this project. The sugar solution can be *very hot.*

2. In a saucepan, mix the water and sugar with the spoon. Ask the grownup to help you place the saucepan on a stove burner and bring the solution to a boil.

3. Reduce the heat to medium. Continue to boil the solution, stirring it frequently for 5–7 minutes, until the sugar dissolves and the solution is clear. Stir the solution very slowly, being sure not to splash the liquid.

4. Ask the grownup to help you use an oven mitt to remove the saucepan from the heat.

5. Let the solution cool for about 5 minutes.

6. Ask the grownup to help you pour the sugar solution into a glass jar until it's about 1 inch from the top of the jar.

7. Cut a circle from heavy construction paper or cardboard that's large enough to cover the opening of your jar.

8. Use the pointed end of a bamboo skewer to poke a hole through the center of the circle.

9. Set the circle on top of the jar and slide the skewer through the hole and into the sugar solution until the end is 1 inch from the bottom of the jar.

10. Put the jar in a place where it will not be disturbed at room temperature.

Edible Concoctions

11. The next day, sugar crystals will appear on the bamboo skewer. In about 4–5 days, your edible "diamonds" will be ready!

12. Ask the grownup to help you use a fork to scrape the sugar crystals from the skewer and out of the jar.

13. Lay the crystals on a paper towel to dry. Break up any large crystals into smaller pieces using the fork.

Here's How You Use It

Spread corn syrup or Tasty Glue on an edible craft, such as a gingerbread house. Sprinkle the diamonds on the craft. Or use the diamonds to decorate cookies, cakes, and other desserts.

Here's How You Store It

Put the leftover sugar mixture in a plastic bag, then toss the bag into the garbage. Store the diamonds in an airtight container at room temperature for several weeks.

Crafty Idea

Here's how to make a dazzling diamond necklace you can wear then eat:

1. Measure a piece of cotton string long enough to tie around your neck.

2. Place the string in the sugar solution so the middle of the string (about 4–5 inches) is in the solution and the ends hang outside the jar. Push the string down with a fork, but leave about 1 inch of space between the bottom of the string and the bottom of the jar.

3. Cover the jar loosely with aluminum foil. In about 4–5 days, sugar crystals will appear on the string.

4. When the center portion of the string is covered in crystals, remove the string carefully, rinse it under water, and let it air-dry on a paper towel.

5. Tie the sparkling diamond necklace around your neck.

Candy Glass

This sweet treat has a smooth and shiny finish, just like glass. It can be used to make windows for a gingerbread house, edible dishes, or shiny ornaments.

Here's What You Need

Saucepan
Metal mixing spoon
1 cup sugar
½ cup white corn syrup
¼ cup water
4–5 drops food coloring (optional)
Glass of cold water
Oven mitt
¼ teaspoon vanilla extract
Baking sheet
Cooking spray
Plate

Here's How You Make It

1. Ask a grownup to help you with this project. The sugar solution can be *very hot*.

Grownup Help

2. In a saucepan, use the spoon to mix the sugar, corn syrup, and water. If you want colored candy glass, stir in the food coloring.

3. Ask the grownup to help you place the saucepan on a stove burner and bring the mixture to a boil.

4. Reduce the heat to medium. Continue to heat the solution, stirring it frequently for about 8 minutes. Stir the solution very slowly, being sure not to splash it.

5. Test the temperature of the solution. Spoon a drop of the solution into a glass of cold water. If the drop hardens, then ask the grownup to help you use an oven mitt to remove the saucepan from the stove. (If the drop stays soft, keep the saucepan on the heat for an additional 2–3 minutes, then test another drop of solution in another glass of cold water. If the drop hardens, remove the saucepan from the heat.)

6. Immediately stir the vanilla into the solution.

Here's How You Use It

1. Spray a baking sheet with cooking spray.

2. Ask the grownup to help you pour the solution carefully into circles on the baking sheet.

3. Let the candy harden for 10–15 minutes.

4. Carefully remove the candy glass from the baking sheet.

5. You can leave the candy glass as circles, or you can break it into rectangles, squares, and other shapes.

Here's How You Store It

Store the candy glass in a single layer on a plate in the fridge for several weeks.

Crafty Idea

Here's how to make edible ornaments:

1. Loop a 6-inch piece of string or thread and tie the ends together.

2. Spray a metal cookie cutter with cooking spray. Place the cookie cutter on a piece of aluminum foil sprayed with cooking spray. Wrap the sides of the aluminum foil up and around the cookie cutter.

3. Set the cookie cutter on a baking sheet, and pour the solution into it.

4. Immediately use a Popsicle stick to poke about ½ inch of the looped string or thread gently into the solution at the top portion of the cookie cutter.

5. After the candy glass hardens, use the looped thread to hang your edible creation.

Tasty Glue

This tasty, edible glue is perfect when you need to stick pieces onto gingerbread houses or other edible crafts. It also works well for gluing paper.

Here's What You Need

Small saucepan
1 tablespoon cornstarch
⅓ cup cold water
Mixing spoon
1½ tablespoons Jell-O mix
1 tablespoon corn syrup
Oven mitt
Popsicle stick
Airtight container or Ziploc bag

Here's How You Make It

1. In the saucepan, mix the cornstarch and cold water with the spoon.

2. Add the Jell-O mix and corn syrup.

3. Ask a grownup to help you place the saucepan on a stove burner and bring the mixture to a boil.

4. Ask the grownup to help you stir the mixture until it's thick and gel-like.

5. Ask the grownup to help you use an oven mitt to remove the mixture from the heat.

6. Let the glue cool slightly before you use it.

Here's How You Use It

Spread the glue with a Popsicle stick to glue edible or paper crafts.

Here's How You Store It

Store the glue in an airtight container or Ziploc bag at room temperature for up to 1 week.

Edible Concoctions